OSCAR WILDE

David Pritchard

GEDDES&GROSSET

This edition published 2001 by Geddes & Grosset,
an imprint of Children's Leisure Products Limited

© 2001 Children's Leisure Products Limited,
David Dale House, New Lanark ML11 9DJ, Scotland

ISBN 1 84205 051 6

Printed and bound in Scotland

CONTENTS

	I	The Early Years	9
	II	University Education	26
	III	The Path to Wealth and Fame	42
	IV	Touring the United States of America	57
	V	Bachelorhood, Marriage and Other Relationships	72
	VI	The Man of Masks	87
	VII	Return to the Theatre	102
	VIII	Impending Disaster	116
	IX	The 'Wilde Scandal'	132
	X	Imprisonment	151
	XI	The Final Years	165
		Afterword	178
		Chronology	183

CHAPTER I

*T*HE EARLY YEARS

Few men have ever made such an impression in one short lifetime as Oscar Wilde. For good or for ill, he imprinted himself so strongly on his contemporaries that before his death at the early age of forty-six he had attained almost mythical proportions in their eyes. Wilde's rise to social and artistic prominence, subsequently followed by his spectacular fall into disgrace, was unequalled. Yet, although supremely individual in everything he did, he inherited both his virtues and his vices from his Irish forebears. Through their blood-lines came the seeds of the genius that brought Oscar to the heights of literary and popular fame. Equally they bequeathed to him a fatal streak of reckless arrogance, a quality which led him to fall like one of Milton's rebel angels from Heaven to the pits of a personal Hell.

Oscar Wilde was the most notable member of a remarkable family. His father, Sir William Wilde, made his mark on nineteenth-century Ireland as a doctor, scholar and writer. His mother, Jane Francesca Elgee, was the poet 'Speranza', whose patriotic verses helped inspire the literary rebels of the Young Ireland movement. Many years later, following her death in 1897, Wilde acknowledged his debt to both his parents in 'De Profundis'. 'No one knew how deeply I loved and honoured her. Her death was terrible to me, but I, once a lord of language, have no words in which to express my anguish and my shame. She and my father had bequeathed me a name they had made noble and honoured, not merely in literature, art, archaeology and science, but in the public history of my own country, in its evolution as a nation.'

Oscar Wilde's mother and father were leading members of the Anglo-Irish Protestant elite. His father's family could be traced back to the town of Walsingham in County Durham, where they had worked for generations as artisans and builders. Around 1750 one Ralph Wilde decided he should leave Walsingham and try his luck in Dublin. The great eighteenth-century building boom that turned the old medieval town into a great Georgian city was in progress, and the young man hoped to make his fortune. Ralph Wilde thrived in his new surroundings, became a rich merchant and raised a large family with his Irish wife. One of his sons, also named Ralph, was particularly ambitious and succeeded in gaining the position of land agent at Castlerea, the great County Roscommon estate of Lord Mount Shannon. He married a local woman, Margaret O'Flyn, and fathered three sons, Ralph, William and Thomas. Ralph went to Dublin, where he became a clergyman and a highly respected Greek scholar, whilst William emigrated to the West Indies to make his fortune in the lucrative sugar trade. But Thomas Wilde returned to his birthplace after studying medicine in Dublin, and spent the rest of his long life as a doctor in Roscommon and Mayo.

Thomas Wilde, like his father before him, married into one of the distinguished Irish families of Connaught. His wife Emily was a member of the noted Fynnes of Ballymagibbon, near Cong in County Mayo. Fynne, curiously enough, translates into English as wild, and these Irish ancestors of Oscar's lived up to their names. They were notoriously eccentric, and many tales were told about their strange doings. John Fynne, Thomas's father-in-law and Oscar's great grandfather, was a religious fanatic, and spent much of his fortune in attempts to bribe his Catholic tenants to convert to the Protestant faith. The aristocratic Fynnes rather looked down on Emily's bourgeois doctor husband, but nevertheless Thomas Wilde did well in his chosen profession. He established a lucrative medical practice in Mayo and Roscommon, from the proceeds of which he raised and educated three successful sons.

William Wilde, the father of Oscar, was born to Thomas and Emily at Kilkeevin, County Roscommon in 1815. From a very young age it was his desire to follow the medical profession, and in 1832 he left Roscommon to study at Dr Steevens's Hospital in Dublin, where Dean Swift had once been governor. William Wilde's abundant energy and intellectual talents quickly brought him great success in medicine and several other fields of endeavour. Within a year of beginning his studies he played an important part in suppressing a cholera epidemic in his native Connaught, and in time he became one of Dublin's leading medical consultants. His area of expertise was ocular and aural (eye and ear) surgery, but his exceptional organizational skills were put to use on more than one occasion by the English administration that governed Ireland. Wilde's greatest achievement in this field came in 1852, a few years after the end of the Great Potato Famine, when he undertook a statistical survey of the diseases that were afflicting the Irish population after years of starvation. Wilde's career as a surgeon made him a wealthy man, and he set up his home and surgery in Merrion Row, at the heart of Dublin's most fashionable quarter.

William Wilde was a man with a wide range of interests, and followed many intellectual pursuits outside medicine. Although sympathetic to the cause of Irish freedom, he was no revolutionary, and his nationalist sympathies were directed to Ireland's past rather than her present. He was a leading light in the antiquarian movement of the era, which included the artists George Petrie and Frederick William Burton. Wilde wrote important articles on lake dwellings and other aspects of prehistoric Ireland, as well as amassing a large collection of folklore tales from his Irish patients that would be published after his death by his wife. His greatest single contribution in this field came in 1857, when he undertook to catalogue the archaeological treasures in the Royal Irish Academy for a permanent exhibition that was to be held in Dublin. Within four months he had accomplished the first part of this huge task, which had defeated the efforts of a committee for over three years. In 1862 he completed the third and final volume of the catalogue, a feat for which he received international acclaim and the Order of the Polar Star from King Charles XV of Sweden. These activities, along with his many books (most famously *Lough Corrib* and *The Closing Years of Dean Swift's Life*, made William Wilde one of the most highly regarded literary and cultural figures in Ireland. There was, however, a less reputable side to his character. He was as energetic in the bedroom as in all his other pursuits, and was reputed to be a notorious libertine. Wilde is known to have fathered at least four illegitimate children by several different women; one of his sons, Henry Wilson, he brought into his medical practice and trained as his assistant. He had two daughters, Emily and Mary, by another woman, who were brought up by his clergyman brother Ralph. They died tragically in their early twenties at a house party in Monaghan, when their dresses caught fire as they waltzed close to an open fire. William Wilde's sexual excesses, like those of his famous son, would eventually destroy his reputation and blight the closing years of his life.

In appearance William Wilde was a fairly short, slightly built man, with an unkempt mane of hair and grimy-looking olive-coloured skin. It was odd that his choice of bride should be a woman who was his physical opposite. Jane Francesca Elgee came from a long-established family of landowners in County Wexford. According to family tradition the Elgees were of Italian descent and their name was an Anglicization of Algiati, belonging to one of the great merchant families of Florence. Jane Elgee embroidered this claim to include the poet Dante in her family tree, but in reality the Elgees more likely derived from the more mundane Aljoys, whose Scottish ancestors settled in County Louth during the fifteenth century. The parents and relatives of Jane Elgee, whatever their origins, were the typical nineteenth century Anglo-Irish mix of landowners, clergymen and the professional classes. Her own father was a successful lawyer. The one artistically noteworthy family member was Jane's uncle, the writer Charles Maturin. Today he is almost forgotten, but his Gothic novel *Melmoth the Wanderer* was one of the most famous books of its time, and inspired a sequel by the French novelist Balzac. Oscar, following his release from prison and exile to France in 1897, was to hide himself under the pseudonym Sebastian Melmoth, the name of his uncle's most famous fictional creation.

Jane Elgee was probably born in December 1821, although she invariably gave her birth date as 1824 or later. She grew up to be a towering, rather plain woman, with a tendency to run to fat and a somewhat mannish voice. Despite these physical deficiencies she lacked neither self-confidence nor the ambition to make a name for herself. In 1846 Jane came to Dublin and became associated with the revolutionary Young Ireland movement. Like others in her social class she had been horrified by the effects of the famine on the Irish peasantry, and believed that English rule must be overthrown through rebellion. John Mitchel, the most radical of the Young Ireland leaders, had recently broken away to edit *The United Irishman* in competition with the more restrained nationalist newspaper *The Nation*. Jane Elgee began contributing inflammatory poems and ballads to be published in these journals, and through her literary efforts established a lifelong reputation as a poet and patriot. Her verse was of little artistic merit, but its bloodthirsty call to rebellion and mayhem established her as a heroine of the nationalist movement both in Ireland and the United States. In 1848 the authorities suppressed the Young Ireland movement, and charged Mitchel and its other leaders with treason; they were tried and afterwards transported to Australia as convicts. Jane Elgee, perhaps because of her sex and her Anglo-Irish background, was spared their fate and remained in Dublin without hindrance from the government. In 1851 she married William Wilde, who had been courting her for some time, and settled into the house in Merrion Row. There she and her husband entertained the intellectual cream of Anglo-Irish society, including such luminaries as the mathematician William Rowan Hamilton, the poet Samuel Ferguson and the novelist Charles Lever.

William, the Wildes' first son, was born in 1852, and by 1854 Jane was pregnant again. She would have liked a girl for her second child but this was not to be. The son she bore would more than compensate for any disappointment she might have felt at the time. Oscar Fingal O'Flahertie Wills Wilde was born at 21 Westland Row, Dublin, on 16 October 1854. In later years he joked that he should have been called 'The Oscar' or 'The Wilde' but it was apt that such a big man should carry a name that was out of the ordinary. 'Oscar' celebrated one of the Celtic heroes of the Fenian cycle of tales, although it may also have been a compliment to King Oscar I of Sweden, who was said to be one of Wilde's patients. 'Fingal' and 'O'Flahertie' reflected Sir William's Galway origins and his Irish relations, whilst 'Wills', the last of the middle names, was given in deference to one of the doctor's distant relatives, a playwright who had shown him particular kindness over the years.

The early years of Oscar Wilde, like those of any child, can be traced only in flashes and half-memories. Speranza later claimed that she dressed him as a girl until he was ten years old, but she was always a notorious exaggerator and this seems unlikely. Certainly, as was the custom in Victorian times, he wore dresses for the first years of his life. There is a famous photograph of Oscar aged about four, in which he is wearing a ball gown and has his hair in bangs, but this is deceptive. The Wilde's next child, Isola, was a girl, and it seems unlikely that Jane would have wanted to keep her second son as a surrogate daughter. In fact, contrary to the picture that many biographers have given of his childhood, Oscar was by no means his mother's favourite in his early years. In a letter of June 1855 she described him as 'a great stout creature who minds nothing but growing fat', whilst her eldest son Willie was 'light, tall and spiritual, looking with large, beautiful eyes full of expression. He is twined round the fibres of my heart.' In another letter of February 1858 she describes Willie and Oscar as 'growing tall and wise', but ten-month old Isola as 'the pet of the house'. She has fine eyes and promises to have a most acute intellect'.

Most of the stories that survive about Oscar's early years suggest he was a normal boisterous infant, with a knack for getting into minor scrapes. On one occasion he broke his arm playing rough games with his brother and a friend; on another, whilst on holiday, he hid in a cave and there was a general panic until he was found. His summers were spent in his father's hunting lodge in Galway, in the Wicklow Mountains, or by the seaside in Dungarvan, County Waterford. According to one story, probably apocryphal, it was on Dungarvan beach that he met and became friendly with Edward Carson, who would one day be his rival in Trinity College, and later again cross-examine him in the Lord Queensberry libel case. In 1855 William Wilde moved with his family to a much larger house at 21 Merrion Square, just around the corner from Westland Row. In these comfortable, if often untidy, surroundings Oscar spent most of his formative years. Speranza ran a Bohemian and rather risqué household by the standards of the era, and seems to have entered into an unspoken agreement with William to turn a blind eye to his mistresses. She continued to entertain the intelligentsia of Dublin at her salon, but spent much of her time lying in bed. The children were privately tutored at home, and encouraged to converse in French and German as well as English. It was a pleasant existence, and until Oscar's enth year few passing clouds seem to have troubled the unconventional lifestyle of the Wildes. But then the sky darkened, and because of Sir William's reckless amorality, Speranza and her brood would find themselves at the centre of a storm of controversy.

By the early 1860s William Wilde was at the pinnacle of his career, having just received a knighthood for his many achievements in public life. Then, in 1862, he launched on a disastrous sexual liaison with a much younger and possibly insane patient, which brought him into ridicule and disrepute. Mary Josephine Travers, the object of his affection, came from the same social class as Wilde. He was to find that she could not be bought off as easily as most of his other mistresses. The doctor himself seems to have abandoned his usual discretion, and openly paraded his new prize around the city, to the great annoyance of his long-suffering wife. At length – after she was rumoured to have stumbled on the adulterous couple cavorting in her bed – Speranza put her foot down and told Sir William to get rid of the girl. This proved to be harder than he expected. Mary Josephine Travers was neurotic, and in her demented opinion had good cause to hate the surgeon and his wife. She embarked on a campaign of revenge on Sir William, and published a pamphlet describing her seduction at his hands. Miss Travers wrote her diatribe under the pseudonym Florence Boyle Price, but to make sure nobody missed the point distributed it as coming from the pen of Speranza. The pamphlet tells how Wilde (or 'Quilp' as she calls him) doses her with ether during a medical consultation, and then rapes her whilst she is half conscious. Following a later confrontation with the doctor, in which he reveals his evil nature ('I will turn the tables on you now – you are

17

now in my power. If you breathe a syllable of the chloroform you blast yourself by revealing it.'). Florence turns to Mrs Quilp (Speranza) for help, but is turned away from her door. At the end of the pamphlet Mary Travers included a selection of Wilde's love letters to her, and openly challenged her ex-lover to sue her if he wanted to clear his name.

Wilde's response was to try and buy off the woman with money to go to Australia, where her brothers were living. Mary Travers played him along, but had no intention of going anywhere until the hate campaign had destroyed the man who so casually rejected her. She began stuffing scurrilous verses through the letterbox at 21 Merrion Row, like this one insulting Sir William's brood of illegitimate children:

> 'Your progeny is quite a pest
> To those who hate such "critters"
> Some sport I'll have, or I'm blest
> I'll fry the Wilde breed in the West
> Then you can call them "Fritters".'

Speranza was eventually forced to flee with her children to the seaside town of Bray in a futile effort to escape from her husband's tormentor, but Travers followed her there and laid siege to the house where the family were staying. At length Speranza could stand no more, and wrote a letter to the woman's father, the professor of Medical Jurisprudence at Trinity College.

'Tower, Bray, May 6

Sir – You may not be aware of the disreputable conduct of your daughter at Bray, where she consorts with all the low newspaper boys in the place, employing them to disseminate offensive placards, in which my name is given, and also tracts, in which she makes it appear that she has had an intrigue with Sir William Wilde. If she chooses to disgrace herself that is not my affair; but as her object in insulting me is in the hope of extorting money, for which she has several times applied to Sir William Wilde, with threats of more annoyance if not given, I think it right to inform you that no threat or additional insult shall ever extort money for her from our hands. The wages of disgrace she has so loosely treated for and demanded shall never be given her – Jane F. Wilde.'

In writing this letter Speranza blundered, and played into the hands of her husband's nemesis. When Mary Travers acquired the letter from her father, as was inevitable, it gave her grounds to take a libel case against the Wildes. The case, when it came to court in December 1864, provided one of the juiciest sex scandals Victorian Dublin had ever enjoyed. To add to Speranza's sense of injury the main barrister on the plaintiff's side was Sir Isaac Butt, a long-time friend who had once been her lover. Mary Travers' account of her forced seduction in Wilde's surgery ('She went in a maid, that out a maid never departed more' as one of her lawyers described it) was taken with a large grain of salt by almost everybody in the courtroom. She was seen for what she was, a spiteful rejected mistress who had gone to insane lengths to pay off a grudge against her former lover. Speranza testified in defence of her husband, and made a generally good impression on the jury, although she over-egged the pudding when she claimed that she believed her husband had never been sexually involved with his accuser. Whilst it was loyal of her, it was also the most blatant perjury. At the end of the trial the jury awarded Mary Travers a farthing's damages, which was all they thought her virtue and good name were worth. Unfortunately for Sir William he was left to pay £2,000 in legal damages, and found himself the laughing stock of Dublin. The loss of face, to such a proud and even arrogant man, was worse than the financial loss, and the surgeon never fully recovered his earlier buoyancy.

It is difficult to know how much these events impressed themselves on the young Oscar Wilde, especially since by the time of the trial he was at school. Perhaps he saw the scandal through the eyes of his mother, who refused to acknowledge the damage Mary Travers had caused, and closed her eyes to the truth that the shameful behaviour of her husband had provoked the crisis. One thing is certain. Neither Oscar nor Speranza took in the most important lesson of the libel action, which is that you should never sue somebody unless you are blameless yourself. Just over thirty years later Oscar Wilde would find himself in a similar situation to Mary Travers, and choose to take a libeller to court. And Oscar would lose because the accusation against him was substantially true.

It may or may not have been coincidental that, as the Mary Travers affair approached its sordid climax, both Oscar and his brother Willie were packed off to boarding school. In later years, when he was a famous public figure, Wilde talked down this experience, and left his listeners with the impression he had only spent a year or two in formal education, and mainly been tutored privately. His reasons are not different to understand. Portora, the public school in Enniskillen,

County Down, where he was sent at the age of ten, was one of the most prestigious schools in Ireland. It liked to call itself 'the Eton of Ireland', but compared to the great English public schools the institution was a mere learning factory for the Anglo-Irish middle-classes. No self-respecting aesthete and ambitious social climber like Oscar would want to be closely associated with anything but the most aristocratic schools in the country. He preferred to let the world think he had learnt his Greek and Latin at the feet of some erudite but anonymous private tutor.

This was probably a harsh judgement on Portora School, which provided a fine grounding in the classics for its lazy but brilliant new student. The recollections of Wilde's schoolmates suggest that he was popular, gregarious and already possessed much of the easy-going charm that became his trademark in later years. Oscar, according to the memoir of one friend, was a dandy even at this early age, and had taken to wearing a silk top hat to school. He was honing his conversational skills, and could embroider the everyday incidents of school life into epic tales of courage and defiance, usually with himself as the central figure. He suggested nicknames for most of his friends at school, and they retaliated by calling him 'The Grey Crow', a name that he seems to have cordially disliked. Nonetheless, he surely preferred his soubriquet to Willie Wilde's. His elder brother had inherited his father's 'dirty' olive skin, and was told one day his neck was filthy. He responded by protesting it was only the aristocratic blood of his family showing through his skin, and for the rest of his school career Willie carried the name 'Blue-Blood'.

Whilst the younger of the Wilde brothers did not shine at most of his schoolwork, he had prodigious abilities when it came to reading. Oscar later claimed that he could read a three-volume novel in a half-hour as a schoolchild, and absorb two or three books simultaneously. One of his most unusual characteristics, both at school and at college, was his hatred of sports. This was contrary to the whole ethos of Victorian education, which stressed that the exercise of the body was as important as the development of the mind. But Oscar simply refused to participate in the athletic and team games at Portora. He was a big child, but slow and a little clumsy. Because of his natural laziness, or perhaps his reluctance to participate in activities where he could not excel, the child avoided the playing fields on every occasion. In this aspect of his school life, as in many others, Oscar lagged behind the achievements of his more athletic and diligent elder brother. Nevertheless, some of his unique qualities were beginning to surface, since Speranza commented to an acquaintance 'Willie is alright, but as for Oscar, he will turn out something wonderful.'

In 1867 Oscar Wilde faced tragedy for the first time in his life, when his nine-year-old sister Isola suddenly died of a fever. Speranza and Sir William were devastated by the loss of their youngest child, who was the much-pampered pet of the family. Oscar, a dreamy romantic child who idolized his sister, was almost as distraught as his parents. He was given a lock of her hair, and placed it in an envelope, which he decorated with religious mottoes, crosses and their intertwined initials. When he died in Paris the envelope and its lock of hair were found amongst his few remaining possessions. In later years Oscar re-visited Isola's grave, and wrote a simple but quite beautiful poem, 'Requiescat', in her memory.

'Tread lightly, she is near
Under the snow,
Speak gently, she can hear
The daisies grow.

All her bright golden hair
Tarnished with rust,
She that was young and fair
Fallen to dust.

Lily-like, white as snow,
She hardly knew
She was a woman, so
Sweetly she grew.

Coffin-board, heavy stone,
Lie on her breast,
I vex my heart alone,
She is at rest.

Peace, Peace, she cannot hear
Lyre or sonnet,
All my life's buried here,
Heap earth upon it.'

The death of Isola was one of the most important incidents of Oscar Wilde's childhood, and may have contributed to the deep vein of sadness that lay concealed beneath the glittering personality of his maturity. But life went on, and in time he put the tragedy to one side and turned his mind to his education and future career. Oscar's intellectual talents came to the fore during his last two or three years at Portora. He developed an interest in the Greek language, a subject that was to dominate his academic interests for some years to come. Today the study of the language and culture of classical Greece is an educational backwater, and not seen as relevant to our society and culture. But in the nineteenth century it was considered the noblest and most important subject in the school curriculum. Greek philosophy and science provided a standard of excellence by which the Victorians measured their own aspirations, whilst Athens was held to be the model of a near perfect society. Greek was further revered as the language of the gospels and the other early Christian scriptures.

Oscar was deeply affected by his own discovery of the lost civilization of the ancient Greeks. His interest in their culture and language endured throughout his life, and coloured his opinions in almost everything he did. In 'De Profundis', his long prison letter to Lord Alfred Douglas, Wilde wrote of the Greek language as the medium through which he could read the living words of Christ.

'Of late I have been studying the four prose poems about Christ. At Christmas I managed to get hold of a Greek testament, and every morning, after I had cleaned my cell and polished my tins, I read a little of the gospels, a dozen verses taken by chance anywhere ... When one returns to the Greek it is like going to a garden of lilies out of some narrow and dark house. And to me, the pleasure is doubled by the reflection that it is extremely probable we have the actual terms used by Christ. It was always supposed that Christ talked in Aramaic. But now we know that the Galilean peasants, like the Irish peasants of our own day, were bilingual, and that Greek was the ordinary language of intercourse all over Palestine, as indeed all over the eastern world. I never liked the idea that we knew of Christ's words only through the translation of a translation. It is a delight to me to think that as far as his conversation was concerned, Charmides might have listened to him, and Socrates reasoned with him, and Plato understood him.'

Wilde was lucky in his Greek teachers at Portora, who nurtured and fostered his newly found scholarly instincts. One of them, J. F. Davis, was an expert on Greek drama. He introduced his impressionable young student to the works of Aeschylus, and the playwright's 'Agamemnon' profoundly impressed Oscar. His enthusiasm for the tragedy encouraged him to study harder, and he rapidly outstripped the best Greek scholars in his class. In 1870 Oscar was awarded the Carpenter Prize for Greek Scripture, and in 1871 (his final year at school) was one of three pupils awarded a Royal School scholarship to Trinity College, Dublin. It was an achievement any developing young classicist could be proud of, and Wilde faced the academic and social challenges of university life full of confidence, and with his belief in his own great destiny reinforced.

CHAPTER
II

UNIVERSITY EDUCATION

Trinity College, which Oscar entered in 1871, liked to consider itself the third great British university after Oxford and Cambridge. In reality it was parochial compared to these great institutions, although it could boast some fine Greek scholars in the ranks of its academics. The young freshman had some advantage over his classmates, since he had literally lived around the corner from the college for most of his life, and was familiar with many of the more brilliant members of its staff through his mother's literary salon. His brother Willie was also attending Trinity, although he would leave during the following year to study law in London. Wilde had other school friends and acquaintances amongst the undergraduates at the college. One of his contemporaries was Edward Carson, and after their confrontation in the Lord Queensberry libel action Wilde stated that they were once good friends, and would promenade around the college grounds arm in arm. Carson, on the other hand, denied that he and his future adversary were ever particularly close, and one is inclined to believe him. Oscar liked to embroider his stories for dramatic effect, and even as a student his attitudes and interests were diametrically opposed to those of the serious and politically ambitious Carson.

At sixteen Oscar Wilde was a striking-looking character, and quite a dandy. He had yet to grow his hair long, but at six foot three he towered over most of his peers. Yet in many ways he was still an awkward schoolboy, and his romantic nature was at odds with the robustly athletic ethos of his fellow Anglo-Irish students. At Trinity he began to develop an interest in the Aesthetic movement, for which he would become a spokesman when he went to Oxford University. Yet at this point in his life his character was by no means fully formed, and he was much influenced by two of his professors, who served as role models and mentors for the embryonic savant.

The Rev John Pentland Mahaffy, Oscar's tutor, was renowned for his scholarship, sporting prowess and biting wit. He was born in Switzerland in 1839, but was brought back to their native country by his Irish parents at the age of ten. He entered Trinity in 1855, and embarked on a glittering academic career that encompassed works on modern European philosophy and ancient Egyptian manuscripts as well as Greek studies. At the same time he was one of the best shots in Ireland and a fine cricketer. Mahaffy's abilities as a conversationalist were legendary, and some of his aphorisms – for instance 'An Irish atheist is one who wishes to God he could believe in God'; or 'In Ireland the inevitable never happens, and the unexpected occurs constantly' – are still treasured. It is no wonder that the youthful Oscar fell under the influence of his self-confident and intellectually brilliant tutor, although the professor's rabid Unionism, and his disdain for the Irish and their Catholic religion, must have offended the son of the nationalist Speranza.

In a letter he wrote to Mahaffy in 1893, Wilde praised his

Trinity tutor as the 'one to whom I owe so much personally, my first and best teacher, the scholar who taught me to love Greek things'. Mahaffy reinforced Oscar's belief in the preeminence of Greece over other cultures, and prodded him to pursue his academic studies harder than he might otherwise have done. Mahaffy was preparing his important *Social Life in Greece from Homer to Menander* during Oscar's Trinity years, and he utilized his student's budding literary talent to correct and improve the manuscript, as he acknowledged on the book's publication in 1874. One of the more daring aspects of Mahaffy's masterpiece was the broaching of the taboo subject of homosexuality in ancient Greece. Wilde's love for his own sex had yet to emerge, but he was surely impressed by the Greek idealization of the relationship between a wiser older man and a youthful companion. It was also typical of the era that Mahaffy's readers were shocked by his scholarly discussion of Greek sexual attitudes. The section dealing with homosexuality was dropped from the next edition of the book.

Oscar Wilde's second important teacher at Trinity was Robert Yelverton Tyrrell, another dazzling Hellenic scholar, who had just been appointed Professor of Latin at the age of twenty-five. Tyrrell was quieter and less overpowering than Mahaffy, but excelled the older man in his linguistic knowledge of ancient Greek. He also had literary aspirations, and published a magazine to which Oscar would contribute some of his earliest published poems. Tyrrell was fond of his witty student, and followed his later brilliant career with interest. In 1896, when Oscar was incarcerated in Reading gaol, the professor signed a petition asking for his release, a brave gesture when the prisoner was so widely held in contempt.

The arrogant and self-centred Mahaffy, on the other hand, refused to help his most celebrated ex-student.

The academic aspects of Oscar's life at Trinity College were matched by his growth in other spheres. He still saw much of his parents, although he preferred to take rooms in the college rather than live at home. The Mary Travers fiasco was by now long forgotten, and the house in Merrion Square was again the centre of intellectual life in Dublin. Oscar regularly attended Speranza's 'at homes' and dinner parties. His growing wit, and his ability to speak on a remarkable number of different topics, were commented on by many of his fellow guests. As they grew older his parents' eccentric domestic habits and disregard for the social proprieties had become even more pronounced. 'I want to introduce you to my mother,' Oscar said to a college friend he brought home to the house in Merrion Square. 'Together we have formed a society for the suppression of Virtue.' Sir William's slovenliness had become legendary, and unhygienic practices like tasting the soup at dinner parties with his dirty thumb did not endear him to his guests. Nonetheless Oscar was proud of his independent and freethinking family. Like them he came to have little respect for conventional morality, and learnt to ignore the carping criticisms of less original minds.

Oscar's great literary discovery during his Trinity years was the poet Algernon Swinburne, whose lush and sensual verse made an indelible mark on his own style. Another seminal influence on his growing aestheticism was the critic John Addington Symonds, whose *Studies of the Greek Poets* (1874) emphasized the artistic sensuality of Hellenic culture. The degree of sexual ambivalence in the works of both these

29

writers suggests that Wilde's homosexual tendency, if not openly expressed, was manifesting itself in his intellectual interests.

Oscar's studies flourished under the guidance of his professors, and he was awarded the Berkeley Gold Medal for Greek Composition, the highest award for classical studies in Trinity. He might have stayed at the College to pursue a fellowship in the Classical department after graduating, but in truth he had outgrown the parochial limits of his native city. Like many of Ireland's most brilliant minds he was stifled by the stale provincialism of his homeland, and needed to escape to the wider world outside its narrow constraints. In early 1874 Mahaffy suggested Oscar apply for one of the two classical scholarships being offered by Magdalen College, Oxford, which offered a grant of £95 a year. In June of that year he went to Oxford to sit the competitive examination for the bursaries. He comfortably won his scholarship, and afterwards met his mother in London and accompanied her on a tour of France and Switzerland.

Oscar's success in entering Magdalen College shaped his future career. In 'De Profundis' he wrote without exaggeration that 'the two great turning points of my life were when my father sent me to Oxford, and when society sent me to prison'. There can be little doubt that remaining in Ireland would have eventually stifled his flamboyance, and reduced his great promise to frustrated mediocrity. Within a few decades Dublin was to become the centre of the great literary and artistic revival known as the Celtic Renaissance. But whilst Oscar may have inherited the Irish gift of the gab, his interests did not tend towards the inward-looking Gaelic mysticism of W. B. Yeats or the idealization of peasant culture that was integral to the works of Lady Gregory and J. M. Synge. To become Oscar Wilde it was necessary that he leave the fishbowl of Anglo-Irish Dublin for the open waters of Oxford and London. Only there, at the heart of a great Empire, could he find a suitable audience for his extrovert talents, and a stage to live out the epic tragedy of his life.

Oscar Wilde arrived at Magdalen in the autumn of 1874. The nineteen-year-old student had achieved a fair measure of academic success at Trinity, and impressed himself on his professors and fellow-students as an amusing and quite exceptional character. But in Oxford he was just another provincial undergraduate, with no connections to the intellectual and social elite that ruled the colleges. There was no red carpet laid out for the son of the Dublin surgeon and the minor Irish poet; he would have to make his name at Oxford solely through his own efforts. That he attained a double first degree and became the focus of the Aesthetic movement at Oxford testifies to his ambition and the strength of his personality. Behind Oscar's flamboyance and seemingly languid demeanour, he possessed the intellect and character to excel in any profession he chose to enter. Yet the thought of being a doctor, or a lawyer, or even a don bored him. At Oxford he turned his back on these options, and committed himself to making his name through the pursuit of his artistic and literary interests. His choice would make him one of the most talked-about young men in London high society by the age of twenty-five.

The England of Queen Victoria, over which Oscar achieved a brief cultural dominance, was a far more complex society than is often portrayed. Its ruling philosophy might be called 'muscular Christianity', a rigid acceptance of Biblical morality coupled with a Protestant work ethic and total belief in supremacy of the English over other peoples and cultures. Yet at the same time a constant stream of philosophical, religious and artistic theories challenged the materialism and moral smugness of the era. The universities of Oxford and Cambridge produced the administrators, diplomats and politicians who were the backbone of Victorian society. Simultaneously they nurtured the theological and cultural trends that made the turbulent intellectual life of the nineteenth century so rich. Few of these philosophies were as controversial as the Aesthetic movement. The word 'aesthete', coined by the philosopher Alexander Baumgarten in 1750, reflected the age-old dispute as to whether art and literature have a moral value, or exist purely to please the senses. Aestheticism in nineteenth-century Europe extolled the value of sensual experience, as opposed to the prevalent philosophy that placed ethical restraints on the individual's actions and cultural expression. The aesthetes stressed the value of freedom from convention both in art and life. Their exaggerated devotion to 'Culture', and spurning of orthodox behaviour, alternately amused and scandalized bourgeois Victorian society. The ambitious student who arrived at Magdalen from Ireland in 1874 did not invent this exotic movement, but he became its spokesman and living example. Oscar extravagantly embraced the aesthetic philosophy at Oxford, and it became a springboard that catapulted him into the sort of popular fame nowadays associated with footballers and pop singers.

During his Oxford years Wilde became acquainted with the two art critics who had most influenced Victorian cultural tastes. John Ruskin, the Slade Professor of Fine Arts, was the spiritual father of the medievalist revival in England, which dominated art, architecture and design for much of the era. His writings and lectures inspired the pastiche Gothic and Romanesque building style so loved by Victorian builders, and he was a champion of the pre-Raphaelite school of painters. Ruskin was not an aesthete in his philosophy, since he believed that art should have a moral purpose. Nevertheless, his refined artistic ideals and strong distaste for the drab materialism of Victorian England attracted the young Irishman. Oscar became one of the undergraduate disciples who gathered around Ruskin, and even participated in one of the Oxford professor's pet projects. The Hinksey Road Campaign sought to transform a track between two villages outside Oxford into a flower-bordered country lane, and for several months the un-athletic Wilde rose at dawn to shift earth and paving stones under the direction of his mentor. But he learnt far more than the pleasures of landscape gardening from Ruskin. Shortly after leaving Magdalen he wrote a letter to thank the professor for his guidance and friendship. 'The dearest memories of my Oxford days are my walks and talks with you, and from you I learnt nothing that was not good. How else could it be? There is in you something of prophet, of priest and of poet, and to you the gods gave eloquence such as they have given to none other, so that your message might come to us with the fire of passion, and the marvel of music, making the deaf to hear and the blind to see.'

Walter Pater, the second great Victorian art critic at Oxford, was a fellow of Brasenose College. He looked to the Italian Renaissance for his theories, which were more sensual than those of the ascetic Ruskin. His writings encapsulated the aesthetic creed, in phrases like 'The love of art for art's sake' and 'Art comes to you proposing frankly to give nothing but the highest quality to your moments as they pass'. Oscar was much impressed by Pater's masterpiece *Studies in the History of the Renaissance*, published in 1873, but did not seek his acquaintance until several years later, when Ruskin was away from Oxford. Wilde then became a member of Pater's circle, and learnt much about the history and philosophy of Art from listening to the great man's pronouncements at first hand. Yet Oscar found Pater's shy and introverted personality unattractive, and in later years discounted his abilities both as a writer and a critic. Nevertheless the Oxford don played an important role in the development of the budding aesthete, and introduced him to the artistically splendid and sexually ambiguous world of the Italian Renaissance.

The death of Sir William Wilde in 1876 removed one of the central figures from Oscar's life. The surgeon, who suffered from asthma and gout, had been ailing for several years. Oscar returned to Dublin to be at his father's deathbed, and was surprised to find an unknown, veiled woman sitting by him. It is believed that she was the mother of one of Sir William's illegitimate children, whom Speranza had generously allowed to visit her former lover at the end of his life. Sir William died on 19 April and was widely mourned, despite his eccentricities and scandals. He had endeared himself to the common people of Dublin through his kindness and healing skills, whilst his intellectual achievements as an antiquarian and scholar were substantial. Oscar's relations with Sir William had not always been easy, as is suggested by a comment in *The Picture of Dorian Gray:* 'Children begin by loving their parents; as they grow older they judge them, sometimes they forgive them.' He owed more of his character to his mother than his father, and she had been the predominant figure in his childhood. Nevertheless Sir William's wide-ranging interests, and his disregard for the everyday moral and social conventions, had been a powerful example in his younger son's formative years. Now, for good or ill, the brooding presence of his father was removed from Oscar's life.

When the surgeon's financial affairs were put in order his family had an unpleasant surprise. The settlement of the legal costs in the Mary Travers affair had made heavy inroads on Sir William's capital, whilst his town and country houses carried heavy mortgages. Oscar found that his share of the estate was so depleted that he could not expect to live on his independent means. He returned to Oxford knowing that in future he would have to support himself through his own efforts.

The summer of 1876 was significant in Oscar's life for other reasons. During that year he began a friendship with a fashionable portrait painter named Frank Miles, who lived in apartments in London. Miles brought him in contact with the glamorous world of upper-class English society and introduced him to Lily Langtry and the other great beauties of the day. Equally importantly, the romantically inclined Oxford student fell in love for the first time, when he met an aspiring actress, Florence Balcombe, in Dublin. 'I am just going out to bring an exquisitely pretty girl to afternoon service,' he wrote to his friend Reginald Harding, 'She is just seventeen years old with the most perfectly beautiful face I ever saw and not a sixpence of money.' Wilde's feelings for

Florence seem to have been quite serious, although his love was not fully reciprocated. His presents to his beloved included a watercolour landscape he had painted at his father's country house at Moytura, County Galway, whilst on Christmas Day 1876 he gave her a gold cross with his name on it. The couple kept in contact over the next two years, but in late 1878 he was shocked to discover she had become engaged to Bram Stoker, the Dublin solicitor and theatre impresario who is today remembered as the author of *Dracula*. Oscar wrote to Florence to say goodbye, and asked for the return of his gold cross. 'As I shall be going back to England, probably for good, in a few days, I should like to take with me the little gold cross I gave you one Christmas morning long ago. I need hardly say that I would not ask it from you if it was anything you valued, but worthless though the trinket be, to me it serves as a memory of two sweet years, the sweetest of all the years of my youth, and I should like to have it always with me.'

In later years Oscar kept up a casual acquaintance with Florence, who became a London stage actress, even sending her a copy of his play 'Salome' when it was published in 1893. But it can be suspected that he also bore her some resentment for her casual abandonment of their relationship. In *The Picture of Dorian Gray* he used Florence as the model for the young actress Sibyl Vane, who is driven to suicide when the novel's protagonist breaks off their engagement. Dorian Gray's description of his first sight of Sibyl (appropriately enough acting in a performance of 'Romeo and Juliet') is Wilde's memory of Florence Balcombe: '... imagine a girl, hardly seventeen years of age, with a little flower-like face, a small Greek head with plaited coils of dark brown hair, eyes that were violet wells of passion, lips that were like the petals of a rose. She was the loveliest thing I have ever seen in my life.' But Oscar's homage to his first love in the novel had a sting in its tail. For all of the fictional Sibyl's sweetness, her family name 'Vane' (i.e. vain) is hardly accidental, whilst there is a hidden slur on Florence's acting abilities in Dorian's dumping of her counterpart after a bad stage performance.

Oscar's wooing of Florence may have been hindered by a secret health problem he had brought upon himself. He is believed to have contracted syphilis in his early years at Oxford, according to legend from 'Old Tess' a local prostitute who gave many of the undergraduates their first sexual experience. The disease was treated with mercury in the nineteenth century, and doctors recommended that the patient abstain from sexual activity for at least two years. It was not realized at the time that the mercury cure did not prevent the long-term effects of syphilis, and some biographers have suggested that the disease may have contributed to Wilde's physical decline and early death.

The death of Sir William Wilde removed a major impediment to his younger son changing his religious faith, if he so wished to. Since his childhood Oscar Wilde had been drawn to the Roman Catholic Church, but his father had always frowned on this interest. Sir William's decision to let his son attend Oxford, in fact, was partly influenced by the fear that he would convert to Catholicism if he stayed in Dublin. Oscar was enchanted by the pomp and colour of Roman ritual in comparison to Protestant practices, and found Catholic dogma more in tune with his own theological inclinations. At Oxford, which about twenty years previously had been the birthplace of a great revival in English Catholicism, he was seriously tempted to change his faith. Nonetheless he still held back, perhaps because he knew his sensual and material nature was at loggerheads with his theoretical desire for the asceticism of a religious life. 'If I could only hope the Church would wake in me some earnestness and purity I would go over as a luxury if for no better reason,' he wrote to a friend in April 1877 'But I can hardly hope it would, and to go over to Rome would sacrifice my two great gods "Money and Ambition". '

The high point of Oscar's religious crisis came in 1877. Two years previously he had accompanied J. P. Mahaffy on a tour of Italy, and he was now given an opportunity to revisit that country, and to tour Classical Greece, with his former tutor and several of his students. After arriving in Genoa by train, the party crossed Italy and visited the Byzantine city of Ravenna. They then took ship from Brindisi to Corfu, and travelled overland to Athens, stopping to inspect the ruins at Olympia, which were being excavated by a team of German archaeologists. Following a tour of the classical sites around Athens the group visited Mycenae, where a few months previously Heinrich Schliemann had uncovered a royal graveyard from the time of the Trojan War. Wilde found his visit to the remains of ancient Greece revived his Hellenistic tendencies, and first-hand contact with the achievements of pagan Athenian culture contributed to his doubts about the Catholic Church. Mahaffy's scorn for the religion of Rome was also influential, since the professor, a staunch Protestant, was horrified at the idea of his former student converting.

Wilde, nonetheless, continued on to Rome after the

Greek trip, where he planned to meet several friends belonging to the Roman Catholic faction at Oxford, who had helped fund his trip abroad. One of these acquaintances, David Hunter Blair, was a convert and about to take holy orders. He used his contacts in the Vatican to arrange an audience with Pope Pius XI for Oscar. That such efforts were made to entice Oscar into the Catholic Church tells much of the esteem in which the Irishman was held at Oxford. He was sorely tempted to convert, but the attempts to sway him were eventually unsuccessful. Although Wilde wrote a flood of poems and sonnets with religious themes during his tour, he returned to England without changing his faith. The final blow to his Catholic aspirations may have been financial rather than theological. Henry Wilson, the illegitimate son of Sir William Wilde who had succeeded to his father's medical practice, died shortly after Oscar's return to England. Amongst his bequests he left his half-brother £100, and a half-share in the fishing lodge in Connemara where the Wilde children had spent some of the happiest days of their childhood. There was, however, a condition; Oscar must remain a Protestant for five years. The undergraduate could not afford to look a gift horse in the mouth, and the desire to hang on to this legacy may have ended his flirtation with the religious life.

Oscar, by his final year at Magdalen, had matured into one of Oxford's most outstanding undergraduates. The tall and exotically dressed aesthete, usually holding the lily that was to become his trademark for years to come, was a familiar sight around the quadrangles of the University. Wilde's cultural tastes were fully formed, and his room was considered the best decorated in the College. Oscar had taken to col-

lecting porcelain, and his casual witticism 'I find it harder
every day to live up to my blue china' provoked *Punch* to
publish one of their first caricatures of him. In 1879 a sketch
called 'The Six-Mark Tea-Pot' appeared in the satirical
magazine. It depicted the 'Aesthetic Bridegroom' (who re-
sembled Oscar) and his 'Intense Bride' examining a teapot.
'It is quite consummate, is it not,' he says, to which she re-
plies 'It is indeed! Oh, Algernon, let us live up to it!' Oscar's
rapid wit and conversational skills were already becoming
famous, and at Oxford he had assumed the rhythmic speech
patterns and upper-class English accent that distinguished
his magnificent speaking voice. Whilst his dandyish appearance and outrageous opinions may have enraged the more
conventional of his peers and tutors, Oscar had gathered a
coterie of like-minded friends around himself. He was the
undisputed leader and inspiration of the aesthetically
minded students at the university.

Academically Wilde shone at Oxford, and would leave
Magdalen in 1878 with a double First degree. But this was
not achieved without some difficulty with the college authorities. He stayed away much longer on his Greek trip
than he should have, and as a punishment was sent down for
the rest of the term. During this enforced absence Oscar
went to London, where he wrote his first published piece of
prose, a review of the opening of the Grosvenor Gallery. But
on returning to his studies he had a piece of good fortune
when it was announced that the subject in 1878 for the university's prestigious Newdigate Poetry prize would be Ravenna, the city he had visited in Italy with Mahaffy. The long
poem Oscar wrote for this competition was perhaps his first
major literary work, but like most of his verse it lacked the

spark of originality that marks the truly great poets. The style of 'Ravenna' was curiously outmoded, and recalled Byron and the Romantic poets rather than Swinburne and Oscar's other contemporary idols. Nevertheless the poem could be considered an outstanding achievement for a young man of twenty-four. It was announced as the winner of the Newdigate prize in June 1878. Later in the same month Wilde learnt that he had achieved a First in Greats, after submitting the best examination papers of the year in the opinion of his lecturers. Oscar crowned his glorious final term at Oxford on 26 June 1878, when he recited 'Ravenna' in the Sheldonian theatre, Oxford, to general acclaim. Following these accolades, the world beyond the gates of Magdalen seemed to be waiting at his feet.

CHAPTER III

THE PATH TO WEALTH AND FAME

The young man who completed his studies at Oxford in the summer of 1878 now faced the reality of making a place for himself in the greater order of things. There was money coming his way, but it was tied up in a house in Ireland that must first be sold. In all Oscar Wilde would inherit about £2,500 from his father and half-brother, which was a substantial sum. But he had expensive tastes, and it was barely enough to support the young gentleman about town that he wished to become. His initial hopes of being offered a fellowship at Oxford so that he could pursue an academic career were soon disappointed. Wilde was a brilliant classicist, but his aesthetic leanings had not made him particularly popular with his elders, and his reputation may have hindered his chances of obtaining one of the three classical fellowships that were offered by the various Oxford colleges in 1878. This failure was probably for the best, since he was far too flamboyant to settle comfortably into the enclosed and stifling environment of the Oxford scholars. In his heart Oscar knew this, and when asked by his undergraduate friend Hunter Blair what he would do with his life he replied 'I won't be a dried up Oxford don, anyhow. I'll be a poet, a writer, a dramatist. Somehow or other I'll be famous, and if not famous, notorious.' But his money worries still needed addressing. Whilst Oscar waited for his capital to be realized, he made unsuccessful efforts to obtain a position as an Inspector of Schools.

The obvious path to the wealth and fame he sought lay in the great city of London, where his conversational powers and aesthetic beliefs might bring him the most attention. Wilde had already gained a foothold in the city through his friendship with Frank Miles, and in early 1879 the two men rented a house together at 13 Salisbury Street, off the Strand. From these lodgings, which Oscar ironically named Thames House because it had a very distant view of the river, he set out to ingratiate himself with the capital's upper classes. His plan of attack was simple, and the words of one of the characters in his play 'A Woman of No Importance' aptly mirror his own views. 'To get into the best society, nowadays, one has either to feed people, amuse people or shock people. A man who can dominate the London dinner-table can dominate the world.' Few men could equal Oscar's ability to amuse and shock, and it is fair to say that for years to come he survived not on his wits but by his Wit. In the painter Frank Miles he had a useful ally, since his slightly older co-tenant attracted the best-known actresses and society ladies to his studio in the attic of 13 Salisbury Street. Miles was colour-blind, but it did not stop him being one of the most fashionable artists in England at the time. Many of his society portraits, as well as cloying studies of Victorian working-class girls and children, appeared in the popular magazine *Life*. 'The Flower Girl', one of his most popular works, was the favourite picture of Edward, Prince of Wales. Oscar's opinion of his friend's limited artistic abilities has not been recorded, but with the help of Miles he was soon to be seen at every fashionable social gathering.

Through his social activities Oscar developed ties to the leading English theatrical personalities, and his shameless toadying to the great actresses of the era helped place him firmly in the public eye. 'The only thing worth loving is an actress', he wrote in *Dorian Gray*, and he spent much of his time running after these exotic and glorious creatures. When Sarah Bernhardt arrived in England in 1879, for instance, he rushed to Folkestone to meet her boat, and cast a bouquet of lilies at her queenly feet as she descended onto English soil. Wilde was at the side of 'La divine Sarah' throughout her stay, and she later paid compliment to his kindness, whilst commenting on his lack of sexual interest in her. 'He was a devoted attendant, and did much to make things pleasant and easy for me in London, but he never appeared to pay court.' Wilde had a similar relationship with Ellen Terry, perhaps the most likeable of all the 'Professional Beauties' of the closing decades of the nineteenth century. When she returned to the stage in 1879 to appear in the play 'Charles I', following an absence of several years, Oscar wrote a sonnet praising her performance. They remained friends for many years, and in a second sonnet, composed after seeing Terry play Portia in 'The Merchant of Venice', he lauded her sublime beauty:

> 'For in that gorgeous dress of beaten gold
> Which is more golden than the golden sun
> No woman Veronese looked upon
> Was half as fair as thou whom I behold.'

Many years later Ellen Terry repaid her fervent admirer with a simple gesture that reflected the unforced kindness of her nature. Near the end of Oscar Wilde's life, when he was an impoverished and ostracized exile in Paris, she chanced to see him on the street one day. He was staring hungrily into the window of a cake shop. Instead of snubbing the dishevelled outcast, as was the habit of most of his former acquaintances, she instead went up and invited him to join her for a meal.

The closest female relationship forged by Oscar in his bachelor years was with Lily Langtry, the extraordinary woman from Jersey in the Channel Islands who became the idol of all England solely on the strength of her beauty. There was a certain affinity between them, since they were both outsiders trying to breach the walls of London society through their own talents. As Oscar used his wit and intellect to advance himself, Lily utilized her perfect face and magnificent body. Following her arrival in England in 1876, with nothing but a boring yachtsman husband and one black ball gown, she had created a sensation. The 'Jersey Lily' was painted by many of the greatest English painters, most famously perhaps Millais (who blundered and showed her holding a Guernsey Lily in his portrait), and was installed as London's most popular 'P. B.' or Professional Beauty. Oscar probably made her acquaintance through Frank Miles in 1877, and was instantly smitten. Lily was the most stunningly beautiful woman he had ever seen, and in the aesthetic order of things, that exceeded any other human quality. 'Beauty is a form of genius is higher, indeed, than genius as it needs no explanation', he wrote in *Dorian Gray*. 'It is one of the great facts of the world, like sunlight, or springtime, or the reflec-

tion in dark waters of that silver shell we call the moon. I
cannot be questioned. It has its divine right of sovereignty ..
To me beauty is the wonder of wonders. It is only shallow
people who do not judge by appearances.'

Lily Langtry, to her fawning young acolyte, was not simply a woman but an abstract idea. She encouraged his devotion, since although she was exceptionally astute in many
ways she had been deprived of a good formal education. Lily
recognized that the brilliant young aesthete had much to
teach her, and was happy to benefit from his advice on everything from Greek drama to her clothes or the best restaurants in
London. But it is highly unlikely that she seriously considered Oscar as a suitor, as he later pretended to himself and
others. Although her friendship and affection for him were
undoubtedly sincere, she had far richer and more prestigious
targets in her sights. At this stage of her life Lily was essentially an extremely high-class courtesan, busily working her
way to the top of the social heap. Yet when she succeeded in
this quest, and was installed as the mistress of the Prince of
Wales, she repaid Oscar's help by introducing him to her
royal lover. The Prince (who had previously told a friend 'I
do not know Mr Wilde, and not to know Mr Wilde is not to
be known') visited Thames House, thus adding greatly to its
residents' social lustre. Shortly afterwards the Jersey Lily's
husband declared himself bankrupt, leaving her penniless.
She looked around for a way to make her own living, being
far too shrewd to depend on the uncertain generosity of the
temperamental Prince of Wales. Oscar and her other friends
suggested she take acting lessons, and with their encouragement she was soon appearing on the London stage. Lily, unlike Bernhardt and Terry, had limited ability as an actress, but

under the critical eye of Oscar learnt enough of the craft to establish herself as an extremely popular leading lady.

Oscar Wilde had stronger sexual feelings for Lily Langtry than for his other actress friends, but it is debatable whether she had any great desire for him. He celebrated her supreme beauty in 'The New Helen', and in a later poem 'To L. L.' described a passionate encounter on a park bench during which she rejected his advances. Perhaps this incident happened, but as in so many of Wilde's writings about his emotional life, there is something false about the verses. Lily's description of their relationship in her autobiography does not mention any romantic attachment. Whilst nobody can blame Oscar for identifying himself with the most glamorous woman in England, his passion for Lily probably remained muted. Certainly it did not merit the doggerel of 'To L. L.'

> '... Well if my heart must break
> Dear love, for your sake,
> It will break in music, I know,
> Poets' hearts break so.
> But strange that I was not told
> That the Brain can hold
> In a tiny ivory cell
> God's heaven and hell.'

Oscar's vain pursuit of the Jersey Lily contributed to his growing notoriety. 'The Apostle of Aestheticism' was attracting attention everywhere, through his outlandish clothes, scintillating wit and challenging views on the importance of Art. This was the best thing that could happen from Oscar's viewpoint, since the adage that 'There is no such thing as bad publicity' was as true then as now. Many people laughed at the extrovert young dandy; others hated and despised him. No matter what others thought of Oscar Wilde, it was very difficult for them to ignore him. Yet, as the Polish actress Helen Modjeska pointed out, his reputation was far greater than his tangible achievements. 'What has he done, this young man, that one meets him everywhere?' she said. 'Oh yes, he talks well, but what has he done? He has written nothing, he does not sing or paint or act – he does nothing but talk. I do not understand.' It was a valid comment, but considering that Oscar had established himself solely on his conversation, he had done remarkably well in attaining so wide a reputation in such a short time. His rooms in Salisbury Street were a shrine to aestheticism, and contrasted with the shabbiness of the rest of the house. The walls of his drawing room, where he entertained Sarah Bernhardt and his many other famous acquaintances, were lined with white panelling. The floor was covered in rich Persian carpets, and the room was filled with blue china, pre-Raphaelite paintings and a collection of art objects.

Oscar's clothes and appearance helped get him noticed. With his height of six foot three inches (one inch shorter than his brother Willie) he towered above most people. He had grown his brown hair down to his shoulders, and his features, whilst not handsome in a conventional sense, were striking. Lily Langtry, in her autobiography *The Days I Knew,* described his facial appearance at this time. His face was 'so colourless that a few pale freckles of good size were conspicuous. He had a well-shaped mouth, with somewhat coarse lips and greenish-hued teeth. The plainness of his face, however, was redeemed by the splendour of his great, eager eyes.' Wilde's taste in clothes had become equally striking. He always dressed immaculately, but such features as knee-length stockings, velvet frock coats and great flopping collars with loosely knotted scarves tied around them, had not been seen on the streets of London for fifty years. His exotic dress marked him out wherever he went, and became synonymous with the Aesthetic movement he championed so eloquently. 'The costume of the nineteenth century is detestable,' he wrote. 'It is so sombre, so depressing. Sin is the only colourful element left in modern life.'

From 1880 onwards, as one useful side effect of his extravagant public persona, Oscar found himself parodied in magazines, books and stage plays. On arriving in London he had made the acquaintance of James A. McNeill Whistler, the eccentric American who was one of his favourite contemporary artists. Oscar formed an uneasy friendship with the brilliant but notoriously difficult painter, and was with him one day in 1880 when they met the cartoonist George du Maurier. Du Maurier, a former pupil of Whistler's, was much amused by the demeanour and aesthetic pronouncements of Oscar, and began to caricature him in the columns of *Punch* as 'Jellaby Postlewaite, the aesthetic poet'. Over the next few years Du Maurier satirized Wilde under such names as Drawit Milde, Oscuro Wildgoose and Ossian Wilderness, but Oscar took the gentle ragging in good part and remained on friendly terms with his persecutor. Other cartoonists joined in the fun, and the features of the longhaired, foppish aesthete, usually with a sunflower or lily in his hand, became known throughout the length and breadth of England.

In the early months of 1881 Wilde was lampooned in two plays. In the comedy 'The Colonel', by F. C. Burnand, editor of *Punch*, the actor Beerbohm Tree appeared as Lambert Stryke, an effeminate aesthete. A little later in the year Gilbert and Sullivan's operetta 'Patience' opened at the Opera Comique in Drury Lane. By accident or design both the 'Idyllic Poet', Archibald Grosvenor, and the 'Fleshly Poet' Bunthorne, who are the operetta's two male leads, shared many of their traits with Oscar. Archibald Grosvenor wore a Byronic shirt with a velvet beret and breeches (a copy of an outlandish costume Wilde often wore in public), and one of his songs recalled a well-known occasion when Oscar was seen bringing a Madonna lily to Lily Langtry –

'Though the Philistine may jostle, you will rank as an apostle
In the high aesthetic band.
If you walk down Piccadilly, with a poppy or a lily
In your medieval hand.'

Wilde did not altogether forget his literary aspirations during these early years in London. He wrote his first stage play, 'Vera; or the Nihilists', and circulated it around his theatrical acquaintances. 'Vera' was a tale of aristocratic revolutionaries in Russia, loosely based on a historical incident. But it was an odd choice of subject, and the melodramatic plot stretched the drama's credibility beyond even the limits of a Victorian audience. Some of the dialogue, particularly that of the character Prince Paul, hinted at Oscar's flair for writing witty epigrams, but there was generally little leeway for the incisive humour that later proved to be his main strength as a dramatist. Oscar's theatrical acquaintances, not unsurprisingly, showed little interest in staging the play, although he did get the offer of an American production. He was undaunted by its tepid reception, and began planning a second play, 'The Duchess of Padua', a pastiche Jacobean tragedy in blank verse.

A more worthy literary endeavour was the selection of the pieces for *Poems*, the first of the sixteen collections of verse (excluding 'Ravenna' and 'The Ballad of Reading Gaol') that Oscar Wilde published in his lifetime. He had been writing poetry since childhood, and began submitting his work to literary magazines whilst still at Trinity College. Nonetheless Oscar was unable to find a publisher for the anthology, and *Poems* was printed at his own expense. The volume was issued under the imprint of the small publishing firm of David Bogue in April 1881, and sold about 1,200 copies in its first few years. The spectrum of poems selected was quite wide, and ranged from the austere 'Requiescat' to sonnets, lush sensual poems in the spirit of Swinburne, and even a patriotic piece 'Ave Imperatrix'. This last poem, which was probably inspired by the Afghan War of 1879, was a bizarre choice of subject for the Apostle of Aestheticism. One can only guess that it was included in a vain attempt to disarm the potential critics of more sensual poems like 'Hélas!' and 'The Garden of Eros' –

> 'For southern wind and east wind meet
> Where, girt and bound by sword and fire,
> England with bare and bloody feet
> Climbs the steep road of wide empire.
> For not in quiet English fields

Are these, our brothers, lain to rest,
Where we might deck their broken shields
With all the flowers the dead love best.
For some are by the Delhi walls,
And many in the Afghan land,
And many where the Ganges falls
Through seven mouths of shifting sands.'

The critical reception of *Poems* was more than a little mixed. Whilst there was much truth in *Punch's* gentle jibe: 'The Poet is Wilde, but his poetry's tame', other reviewers spurned the book as indecent, or treated it as a lash with which to beat the aesthetic movement. Oscar's enemies used his first collection of verse as an excuse to insult him personally. The wave of criticism of *Poems* culminated in a vicious verbal assault on the volume and its author at a public meeting in the Oxford Union. The secretary of the Union was instructed to return the copy of *Poems* that Wilde had sent him. This was exceedingly petty behaviour, especially as the Union had written to Oscar requesting a signed volume for their library in the first place. The whole sordid business was motivated by little more than jealousy, since a first book of poems by a twenty-six year old hardly merited such attention for any other reason. Yet Oscar's many critics had some basis for disparaging his verse, which was imitative rather than original. Wilde, with his chameleon-like intellect, lacked the originality to produce poetic masterpieces. His poems were bland copies of the styles of his favourite writers of the moment, whether Swinburne and Keats in his early efforts, or Baudelaire and the French Symbolists later on. 'The Ballad of Reading Gaol', written towards the end of his life, is possibly the only important Oscar Wilde poem that can be described as truly individual. His verse, with the exception of a few passages from this last poem and one or two shorter pieces, is almost totally forgotten today.

In Oscar's own words, 'There is only one thing worse than being talked about, and that is not being talked about.' However, he was about to discover that his famous epigram had its downside. Oscar had spent a small fortune on redecorating a house for himself and Frank Miles at Tite Street, in the newly fashionable suburb of Chelsea. He employed his friend Edward Godwin, a leading architect and former lover of the actress Ellen Terry, to oversee the work. The aesthete and his artist friend moved to the new house in July 1880, and were settling in nicely when the controversy surrounding *Poems* reached Frank Miles's father, a clergyman in Nottinghamshire. Canon Miles wrote a letter to his son demanding that he sever his friendship with the notorious Mr Wilde at once, or lose his sizeable allowance. This left Frank Miles in a difficult situation, since he could not survive financially without his father's support. His decision to ask Oscar to leave the shared house in Tite Street led to a permanent split between the two men. Their argument was witnessed by one of the artist's young female models, who heard Oscar ask whether Miles would obey his father's unreasonable demand. When Miles replied that he had no choice, Wilde said: 'Very well, then, I will leave you. I will go now and I will never speak to you again as long as I live.' His anger was not merely at losing his home, or because of the substantial financial loss he had incurred. Whatever Wilde's faults, his loyalty to his friends was absolute. What perhaps he found most galling was the hypocrisy of Frank Miles. The artist, who was throwing him out in the name of morality, had a secret vice of his own. He preyed sexually on the young girls, many of them hardly in their teens, that he employed to pose for his popular sentimental portraits. Wilde had turned a blind eye to these activities, and once even misled the police when they came to the house looking for a missing child he knew was upstairs. It was bad enough to be turned out of his home. For this to happen because the father of a man with the artist's vices thought him a bad moral influence was simply unendurable.

In later years Frank Miles declined rapidly from his brief pinnacle of success. In 1887 his precarious mental health broke down, and he was confined to an asylum, where he died four years later. But it seems that Oscar, who was not a vindictive man by nature, never forgave him for his betrayal over Tite Street. In *Dorian Gray*, published in 1891, Miles is one of the several artists he draws on for the character of Basil Hayward, 'whose sudden disappearance some years ago caused, at the time, such public excitement, and gave rise to many strange conjectures'. In one scene of that book Dorian tells Hayward, who has painted the notorious portrait of him, 'on my word of honour I will never talk to you again as long as I live', an echo of Oscar's own last words to Frank Miles. Eventually Dorian Gray, who is in many ways Oscar's idealization of his younger self, takes out a knife and stabs the artist to death. The author's enduring bitterness towards Frank Miles is reflected in this violent fictional ending to the most significant friendship of his early London years.

For a little while Oscar found refuge with his mother, who had moved to London in 1879 so she could be near him and his brother Willie. She had rented a house in

Ovington Street, and now held court there, with Oscar as the main attraction at her salon. Willie Wilde was already suffering under the burden of Oscar's burgeoning reputation. As a child he had been the more successful of the two brothers, but he now found himself in Oscar's shadow. Willie lacked Oscar's intellectual gifts, and his grotesque efforts to match his sibling made him ridiculous. The brothers were not physically unalike, but the shambling and unkempt Willie had none of his brother's wit, taste or mobility of thought. Willie eventually found employment as a journalist, but for the rest of his life he drank too much, drifted from one disgraceful scrape to another, and embarrassed both his mother and his younger brother. With their ages being so close it can be surmised that envy at Oscar's spectacular successes accounted for at least some of Willie's spectacular failures.

Oscar soon found new rooms, but his financial situation was becoming precarious. He had spent his patrimony too freely, and urgently needed to replenish his dwindling funds. To his good fortune, a new and very lucrative opportunity was presented to him. In September 1881 the operetta 'Patience' had opened in New York, where it enjoyed great public success. The impresario Richard D'Oyly Carte, head of the company that was producing the play, also organized lecture tours. The Aesthetic movement was almost unknown in the United States, and he conceived the idea of bringing Oscar, the supposed inspiration for the popular characters in the musical comedy, over to tour the country. The fees for such lectures were extremely high, in larger cities as much as $1,000 for an hour's work, and Wilde jumped at the opportunity. The trip would also allow him to finalize the plans to stage 'Vera' in New York, a project close to his heart. Oscar sketched out a lecture on a suitably aesthetic subject, and ordered a number of flamboyant costumes from his tailor. His forthcoming transatlantic trip caused much adverse comment in the British press, but an article in the magazine *Truth* of 22 December 1881 accurately predicted the unrelieved success that Oscar would enjoy on the far side of the Atlantic.

'Mr Oscar Wilde is going to the United States at the end of this week in the *Arizona*, having made arrangements to bring out his Republican play 'Vera' there, and during his stay he will deliver a series of lectures on modern life in its romantic aspects. The Americans are more curious than we are to gaze at those whose names, from one cause or another, have become household words, and in this I think they are wiser than we are, for it is difficult to realize the personality of anyone, without actually having seen him. Mr Wilde – say what one may of him – has a distinct individuality, and, therefore, I should fancy that his lectures will attract many who will listen and look.'

On 24 December 1881 Oscar Wilde left England en route for New York. In the previous three years he had risen from obscurity to become one of the most controversial men in the country. He would now attempt to confront and charm a new audience with the aesthetic philosophy and his incomparable wit. Both Oscar and the United States could expect to benefit from the experience of meeting each other.

56

CHAPTER IV

𝒯OURING THE UNITED STATES OF AMERICA

The *Arizona* anchored outside New York harbour on the evening of 2 January. Due to the lateness of its arrival the passenger ship could not dock, and the journalists waiting onshore were frustrated in their hopes of interviewing the 'Apostle of Aestheticism' in time for the morning editions. But the American press used their initiative, and several newspapermen hired a launch to take them out to the ship. The man they met surprised them. They expected Oscar Wilde to resemble the aesthetes in Patience and looked forward to meeting a limp-wristed, lisping real-life version of an Archibald Grosvenor. Instead they found a towering six-foot plus giant, who exuded self-belief and was not shy of flaunting his superior intellect at every possible opportunity. On the following day the reporter of the *New York Tribune* recorded his first impressions of Oscar.

'The most striking thing about the poet's appearance is his height, which is several inches over six feet, and the next thing to attract attention is his hair, which is of a dark brown colour and falls down upon his shoulders. The complexion, instead of being of the rosy hue so common in Englishmen, is so utterly devoid of colour that it resembles putty. His eyes are blue, or a light gray, and instead of being dreamy, as some of his admirers have imagined them to be, they are bright and quick and not at all like those of one given to perpetual musing on the ineffably beautiful and true. Instead of having a small delicate hand, only fit to caress a lily, his fingers are long, and when doubled up would form a fist that would hit a hard knock, should an occasion arise for the owner to descend to that kind of argument.'

Oscar's clothes fascinated the reporters, especially the voluminous fur-trimmed green overcoat that hung down to his ankles. This garment, which he had ordered from his London tailor to keep him warm in the colder American climate, remained one of Wilde's favourite possessions for many years. He is seen wearing it in many photographs, one as late as 1892, and it was only lost to him in 1895, when his brother Willie pawned it behind his back. The American pressmen were equally taken with the aesthete's speaking voice. The *New York Tribune* wrote that:

'One of the peculiarities of his speech is that he accents almost at regular intervals without regard to the sense, perhaps as an effort to be rhythmic in conversation as well as in verse.'

According to the reporter from the *New York World* he accentuated every fourth syllable, producing a strange singsong effect. Later the American writer and stage performer Helen Potter, who heard him lecture, analysed his speech patterns in her book *Impersonations*. 'The disciple of true art speaks very deliberately … the closing inflexion of a sentence or period is ever upward.'

The intrepid handful of newspapermen who went to mock Oscar on the *Arizona* left with the knowledge that they had come upon a rare phenomenon. The posturing fool they had looked forward to deriding was articulate and possessed of a rare intelligence. It did not stop the American press hounding him at every opportunity, but they were also genuinely curious about the aesthetic poet's opinions on art and life. The next morning, when he landed on American soil, Wilde found himself surrounded by reporters. 'The renaissance of beauty is not to be hoped for without strife internal and external,' he informed them. 'There is no end to it; it will go on forever, just as it had no beginning. I have used the word renaissance to show that it is no new thing with me. It has always existed. As time goes on the men and the forms of expression may change, but the principle will remain. Man is hungry for beauty.' He then swept off to the Customs Hall, where he is reputed (there is no contemporary account) to have told immigration officials 'I have nothing to declare but my genius.' Considering that his trunks were filled with copies of *Poems*, which he was bringing as presents for the many American celebrities he planned to visit, the statement was as true literally as symbolically.

Oscar settled into the Grand Hotel, Broadway, and waited to present his first lecture at the Chickering Hall on 9 January. In the meantime he was lionized by New York society. 'It is delightful to be a *petit roi*,' he wrote to the wife of his solicitor George Lewis. 'However if I am not a success on Monday I shall be wretched.' He need not have worried. His curiosity value, rather than 'The English Renaissance', which he chose as the subject of his first lecture, was guaranteed to fill the hall with New York's social and cultural elite. 'I am sure you have been pleased with my success,' he wrote to Mrs Lewis a few days later. 'The hall had an audience larger and more wonderful than Dickens ever had. I was recalled and applauded and treated like the Royal Boy' (a popular nickname for the Prince of Wales). Oscar was invited to the best houses in New York, and admirers approached him whenever he went out. He joked that he was now employing two secretaries. The first one copied his autograph, whilst the second (who was rapidly becoming bald) provided locks of his hair for Oscar's countless female devotees.

America had already discovered the autographed fan photos, and Oscar allowed himself to be photographed by the eminent New York photographer Napoleon Sarony. Curiously, Wilde's manager waived the high fees that were usually paid to celebrities for such sessions, possibly because he realized that the free publicity was worth more than any sum they might receive. Sarony took at least twenty-seven pictures of Oscar, featuring most of the costumes his subject had brought with him from England. The photographs provide the most familiar images of Wilde, with his long centre-swept hair, velvet suits and knee-length breeches. They also cunningly hide his large girth, which is unflatteringly highlighted in a Max Beerbohm caricature of his first American lecture. American cartoonists, like Thomas Nast of *Harper's Bazaar,* were not slow to satirize him in the same fashion, and helped spread his fame across the United States.

One result of Oscar's one-man publicity campaign was the extension of his planned four-month tour. Eventually he gave 140 lectures over 260 days, crossing the United States via the southern states to San Francisco by train, and then returning to New York to finish his tour. He also made two brief forays into Canada. Oscar soon modified his lecture on 'The English Renaissance', which he decided was too weighty to interest his American audiences. He shortened it, made it somewhat less theoretical, and changed the title to 'The Decorative Arts'. Wilde was not a natural orator in the popular style of the era, which involve much arm waving, chest thumping, shouting and melodramatic posturing. Instead he relied on his relaxed and naturally warm personality to win over his audiences, adding small anecdotes and epigrams at will to his standard text. In some cities he was scheduled to lecture twice, so he wrote a second lecture called 'The House Beautiful'. This might best be described as a Victorian precursor to the Ideal Homes catalogue, since it consisted mainly of tips on how to decorate a home, with suggestions on furniture, tableware and ornaments.

Occasionally on his tour Oscar would find himself in a city with a large population of Irish emigrants. To them he was the son of the nationalist heroine Speranza rather than an English aesthetic poet, and his views were sought on the political situation in Ireland. The *Philadelphia Press* asked him to comment on the recent murders of Lord Cavendish and his secretary in Phoenix Park. 'When liberty comes with hands dabbled in blood it is hard to shake hands with her,' Oscar replied. 'We forget how much England is to blame. She is reaping the fruit of seven centuries of injustice.' His words were well received, and whilst resting in San Francisco before the return leg of the tour, he wrote a lecture on the Irish Poets of 1848. This was specifically intended for his Irish-American audiences, and the subject was particularly appropriate since his mother was counted amongst their number.

Wilde's desire to fulfil the expectations of his Irish admirers in the United States raises the issue of how important his nationality was to him. Even though he spent most of his adult life abroad, there can be no doubt that Oscar always considered himself an Irishman. When the play 'Salome' was banned in 1892, for instance, he wrote angrily to the Lord Chamberlain's Office that: 'I will not consent to call myself a citizen of a country that shows such narrowness in artistic judgement. I am not English. I am Irish which is quite another thing.' And some years earlier, in conversation with W. B. Yeats, he commented: 'We Irish are too poetical to be poets; we are a nation of brilliant failures, but we are the best talkers since the Greeks.' Yet if Oscar's view of himself as an Irishman was integral to his character, it had only a passing influence on his development as a writer. He was brought up in a house that treasured his nation's cultural heritage, and sat at the feet of Irish poets like his own mother and Samuel Ferguson. Yet as he entered his manhood he found his literary idols and models elsewhere. These came from Classical Greece and England in his youth, and France in his middle years. There was much of Ireland in Oscar Wilde both as a man and as writer. Nonetheless he was not a literary Irish exile like Joyce or Beckett, and drew the inspiration for his stories and plays from London and Paris rather than Dublin.

Shortly after launching into his lecture tour, Oscar found himself in the midst of a serious public argument that damaged his good name in the United States. W. F. Morse, Richard D'Oyly Carte's manager in the United States, also had the Scottish war correspondent Archibald Forbes on an American lecture tour. Forbes disliked Wilde on sight when they met in New York, but it was decided that the two men should travel together from Philadelphia to Baltimore, where D'Oyly

Carte wanted Oscar to attend the Scotsman's lecture after fulfilling his own engagements in the city. But during the train journey Forbes, who was jealous that he had drawn a much lower attendance to his Philadelphia lectures, began insulting Oscar. The aesthete's vanity was pricked, and he refused to alight from the train at Baltimore, preferring to travel on to Washington. The organizers of the Baltimore lecture were furious, whilst Forbes, stung by Oscar's public snub, retaliated by mocking the aesthete's clothes in a statement to the Baltimore newspapers. Wilde defended himself by claiming he had never intended to attend Forbes's lecture, but after the American press began criticizing his rudeness, he tried to heal the breach. He wrote an appeasing letter to Forbes, but the Scotsman would not be placated and continued his public attacks. Eventually Oscar's solicitor George Lewis, who knew the correspondent well, wrote and asked him to desist as a personal favour. The quarrel simmered down, but Wilde's peevish refusal to visit Baltimore turned the American press against him. Henceforth he found them hostile and blatantly unfair, provoking his comment to a *New York Times* reporter: 'If you survive yellow journalism you need not fear yellow fever.'

Unpleasant although the journalistic backlash may have been, it ensured packed crowds in every auditorium where he appeared. Before the Boston lecture sixty Harvard students trooped into the hall wearing aesthetic clothes and carrying a sunflower. Oscar had been warned in advance, and their prank misfired when he came out wearing conventional evening dress. Edgar Allan Poe, the American writer he most admired, had died some years previously, but whilst in Boston he met Oliver Wendell Holmes and Henry Wadsworth Longfellow. Oscar had already met the great American poet Walt

Whitman, whose 'Leaves of Grass' was well known in England. Oscar charmed the older man, even sharing a bottle of Whitman's notoriously vile elderberry wine. The two poets got on remarkably well with each other, considering the vast differences in their backgrounds and ages. But when it came to discussing his poetry Whitman disagreed with his young visitor's aesthetic philosophy. 'Why, Oscar,' he said, 'it always seems to me that the fellow who makes a dead set at beauty by itself is in a bad way. My idea is that beauty is a result not an abstraction.' In those few words he astutely pinpointed the faults both of aestheticism and of Oscar's own poetry.

As Wilde left the eastern cities, and began his journey across the vast continent, he found much to interest and entertain him. He was well served by his charm, and displayed an easygoing friendliness to the people he met on his travels. The openness of his hosts, and their eagerness to meet him, added to the pleasure of seeing the United States at first hand. There is a genuine excitement in Oscar's letters when he describes his first view of American Indians, or his arrival in St Joseph, Missouri a few days after the famous outlaw Jesse James was gunned down by his friend Bob Ford. In Salt Lake City he was amused by the polygamous Mormon elders, and drew a small diagram of the seating arrangements in the lecture hall, where each man sat surrounded by his bevy of wives. From San Francisco he wrote to a friend that 4,000 people had been at the depot to meet him when he arrived. In Leadville, Colorado, a mining city high in the Rockies, Oscar lectured on the great Italian silversmith Benvenuto Cellini. He visited the fabled 'Matchless' silver mine, dined underground with the miners, and opened a new mineshaft named 'The Oscar' in his honour. That evening he visited the local saloon, where he reported seeing a sign saying 'Do not shoot the pianist, he is doing his best'. Oscar liked the miners of Leadville, whom he described as 'ready, but not rough', and thought their red shirts made them the best-dressed men in America.

Two incidents on Wilde's odyssey from New York to San Francisco and back still excite the imagination. In Louisville, Kentucky, he devoted part of his lecture to the English romantic poet, John Keats, and quoted from the 'Sonnet in Blue'. Oscar was unaware that his audience included a woman named Emma Speed, the poet's niece. She was moved by Oscar's praise of Keats, and invited him to call at her house in the town. After showing her guest many of the poet's manuscripts and letters, Mrs Speed presented him with the original copy of the 'Sonnet in Blue'. Wilde's pleasure at receiving the manuscript of one of his favourite poems may be imagined from his letter thanking her for the gift 'What you have given me is more golden than gold, more precious than any treasure this great country could yield me.' Oscar kept the poem until the auction of his possessions in 1895, when it was sold for the knockdown price of thirty-seven shillings.

The second episode was altogether different, and hints at the almost supernatural prescience that Wilde sometimes displayed in his writings and utterances. In Lincoln, Nebraska, he was taken to see the huge penitentiary that dominated the town. Oscar described the visit in a letter to Helena Sickert, the prominent early feminist, younger sister of the great Victorian artist Walter Sickert.

'They drove me out to see the great prison afterwards! Poor odd types of humanity making hideous bricks in the sun, and all mean-looking, which consoled me, for I should hate to see a criminal with a noble-looking face. Little whitewashed cells, so tragically tidy, but with books in them. In one I found a translation of Dante, and a Shelley. Strange and beautiful it seemed to me that the sorrow of a single Florentine in exile should, hundreds of years afterwards, lighten the sorrow of some common prisoner in a modern gaol, and one murderer with melancholy eyes to be hung they told me in three weeks, spending that interval in reading novels, a bad preparation for God or nothing.'

Wilde's comments were prophetic of his own later experience in Reading Gaol, where his favourite book was Dante's *Inferno*, which he mentioned several times in 'De Profundis'. When describing his re-discovery of religion he wrote of 'This new life, as through my love of Dante I like sometimes to call it.' Elsewhere in the letter he quoted the Italian poet's epigram 'Sorrow marries us to God'.

Wilde arrived back in New York in early October 1881, but he was in no hurry to return to England. He was exhausted, and had been infected with malaria during his travels. As an additional incentive to stay in New York, he discovered that his old friend Lily Langtry was due to arrive for her first American theatrical performances. When the boat docked he was waiting with an armful of lilies to meet her. The reporter of the *New York Times,* who was also present, commented on his appearance:

'He was dressed as probably no grown man in the world ever dressed before. His hat was of brown cloth not less than six inches high; his overcoat was of green cloth, heavily trimmed with fur; his trousers matched his hat; his tie was gaudy and his shirtfront open, displaying a large expanse of manly chest. A pair of brown gloves and several pimples on his chin completed his toilet. His flowing hair and the fur trimming of his coat were just of a shade, and they gave him the appearance of having his hair combed down one side of him to his heels and up the other side.'

Oscar escorted Lily around the city, and introduced her to useful contacts like the photographer Napoleon Sarony. Meanwhile he was pursuing his own theatrical ambitions. He had formed an alliance with an American impresario Steele Mackey, who was planning to open a new theatre on Broadway. Mackey, one of the most brilliant stage managers of the era, introduced such features as folding chairs and a safety curtain into theatres; he is also believed to have opened the first school of acting in the United States. He was looking for new plays to open his theatre, and Oscar suggested he produce 'Vera' and the unfinished 'The Duchess of Padua'. Mackey agreed, and they persuaded the prominent American stage actress Mary Anderson to take the leading role in 'The Duchess of Padua'. Marie Prescott, another well-known actress, agreed to star in the melodrama 'Vera' shortly afterwards. Although Mackey's plans for his theatre later fell through, Oscar was confident his plays would be staged in the near future. He embarked from New York two days after Christmas 1882, about £1,200 richer from tour fees and advances for his plays, and eager to finish writing 'The Duchess of Padua'.

Oscar did not stay long in London following his return from America. Having conquered England and America with his charm and intellect, he now set out to do the same in France. Within a month he was on his way to Paris, where he intended to complete 'The Duchess of Padua' in time for its March deadline. The great city by the Seine was the cultural centre of Europe, its art and literature infinitely more daring and innovative than those of the staid capital of England. 'The great superiority of France over England', as Oscar said, 'is that in France every bourgeois wants to be an artist, whereas in England every artist wants to be a bourgeois.' Shortly after his arrival in the city Wilde met a young English expatriate poet named Robert Sherard, a great-grandson of the poet William Wordsworth. The two men disliked each other on their first meeting, but afterwards Sherard was charmed by Oscar, and accompanied him around the city. The Englishman, who knew the cafés and restaurants frequented by poets and artists, introduced Wilde to the bohemian life of Montmartre. Sherard dedicated his first book of verse to Oscar, and the friendship endured for many years afterwards. He was one of the small group of loyal friends who visited Oscar during his prison sentence. They later became estranged, but after Wilde's death Sherard wrote a number of books about his idol, including the first biography.

Oscar renewed his acquaintance with the actress Sarah Bernhardt during his stay, and met many of the great figures of French literature and art, including Emile Zola, Edmond de Goncourt and Victor Hugo, although the last-named slept through his visit. The aesthete's conversations with the Decadent poets Maurice Rollinat and Paul Verlaine had a much greater influence on his literary development. Oscar was inspired to imitate their style in poems like the 'The Harlot's House', which is said to have its origins in a visit to a Parisian brothel:

'Sometimes a clockwork lover pressed
A phantom lover to her breast
Sometimes they seemed to try to sing.

Sometimes a horrible marionette
Came out, and smoked its cigarette
Upon the steps like a live thing.

Then turning to my love I said
"The dead are dancing with the dead,
The dust is whirling with the dust."

But shen she heard the violin
And left my side, and entered in,
Love passed into the house of lust.'

Fashionable Paris was not as impressed with Oscar as London or New York had been. Edmond de Goncourt was amused by his conversation but thought he looked like a homosexual, whilst the artist Degas described him as having 'the look of an amateur playing Lord Byron in a suburban theatre'. Oscar, perhaps stung by the contempt of his hosts for his ostentatious dress, threw off the external mantle of the aesthete. He disposed of his American costumes, with the exception of his green overcoat, and henceforth wore formal, if beautifully tailored, clothes. He also cut his long locks off, although his new hairstyle, inspired by the busts of the Roman emperors in the Louvre, was scarcely less unusual than its predecessor. These changes reflected the maturing of his ideas about art and literature. The French writers were not afraid to write about subjects that the cultural establishment considered taboo. A generation previously the novelist, Gustave Flaubert, had scandalized French society when he wrote openly of female sexuality in *Madame Bovary*, whilst the Impressionist painters were demolishing the existing precepts of the art critics. As Paris approached the end of the nineteenth century, the accepted cultural boundaries were being pushed back further. Verlaine was publishing poems with openly homosexual themes, and a new sensualism was creeping into art, literature and design. Oscar Wilde had discovered his spiritual home. Paris, from now until his death, would be the muse that inspired his most daring literary efforts, and a refuge from the oppressive stagnation of English society.

Oscar's stay in France was cut short by an unexpected financial problem. Mary Anderson had promised to pay him £4,000 for the completed text of 'The Duchess of Padua'. Oscar managed to find time in his crowded social schedule to complete the play by the end of March, but to his disappointment the actress rejected it out of hand. 'We shan't be able to dine with the Duchess tonight,' he flippantly remarked to his friend Robert Sherard when the telegram from America arrived, but the disappointment must have been crushing. Oscar had given his all to writing the play, which he described as 'the chef d'oeuvre of my youth'. Now all his hopes of becoming a successful dramatist were centred on 'Vera', which was due to go into production in New York that autumn. 'The Duchess of Padua' was not staged in New York until January 1891, after Oscar had published his novel *The Picture of Dorian Gray*. Then it was retitled 'Guido Ferranti' and enjoyed a reasonably successful three-week run at the Broadway Theatre.

The loss of the £4,000 from Mary Anderson forced Wilde to consider his financial situation. He returned to England in July 1883, having previously paid the fare for the penniless Robert Sherard to leave France. Oscar's life in England was about to take a new direction, but later in the year the pursuit of his career as a dramatist led to a final short visit to the United States. In August 1883 Wilde returned to New York, where 'Vera' was in rehearsal and about to be staged. The play opened to a packed house on the night of 20 August, and was initially well received, although the audience thought it far too long. But the newspaper reviews were generally unfavourable, with remarks like 'long-drawn dramatic rot' (*New York Herald*) and 'unreal, long-winded and wearisome' (*New York Times*). There was also some criticism for the weak performance of Marie Prescott in the role of Vera – with which Oscar privately agreed. The gate receipts fell sharply, and after a vain bid to persuade its author to appear in the play as Prince Paul, 'Vera' closed on 28 August. For the moment Oscar was forced to accept the failure of his attempts to establish himself as a dramatist. He said goodbye to his brother Willie, who was working as a journalist in New York, and returned to England. For the next few years he would abandon his theatrical ambitions, and concentrate on other ways of making his living. It was only after turning his pen to journalism, short stories and a novel that Oscar decided to write for the theatre again. But this time his efforts were to establish him as one of the most successful playwrights the English stage had ever known.

CHAPTER V

*B*ACHELORHOOD, MARRIAGE
AND OTHER RELATIONSHIPS

The year 1883 marked an important watershed in Oscar Wilde's life. Over the previous five years he had achieved a dubious kind of fame as an aesthete, and tried to make his name as a dramatist. Yet he had failed to establish a literary reputation, or to establish himself financially in London. The next period of his life would be dominated by his attempts to settle down and make a living through journalism, literary criticism and his own creative fiction. It was a watershed between the glittering social successes and literary failures of his young manhood and his flowering into a great dramatist. On a personal level the next seven years would be overshadowed by the conflict between his heterosexual and homosexual selves. Before resolving the vexatious question of his own sexuality, Oscar would pass from bachelorhood to marriage and eventually the legally dangerous verges of open homosexuality.

Oscar's first need on his return to London from Paris was to earn some money. He discovered that Colonel W. F. Morse, the organizer of his American tour, was in England, and approached him to see if he could undertake a similar tour in England. The Colonel was enthusiastic, and Oscar began appearing in London and the provincial cities to talk on 'Impressions of America' and 'The House Beautiful'. The fees were only a fraction of those paid in America, and he rarely received more than twenty-five guineas for a lecture. Nevertheless it provided some source of income to set against his heavy expenditure. Wilde's choice of subjects reflected his own experiences and interests, but they were also designed to appeal to his audiences. The English had fallen in love with the American Frontier, an affair that was to culminate with the arrival in London of Buffalo Bill's Wild West Show in 1886. Queen Victoria's visit to Earl's Court to see the pageant marked the end of her long period of mourning for her husband, Prince Albert. The English were eager to hear about the United States, and flocked to hear Oscar's own slightly ironical views on that country.

'The House Beautiful', on the other hand, was less popular with English audiences. Since setting aside the peacock garb of the aesthete, he had lost much of his value as an object of curiosity. Wilde's ideas on interior design were sound, and made much common sense, but the subject was not appealing enough to fill an auditorium. The *Truth* newspaper, noting the small numbers at his first London lecture, printed a long article, 'Exit Oscar', suggesting his brief period of fame was over. Wilde replied that 'if it took three columns to prove that I was forgotten, then there is no difference between fame and obscurity', but it was true that his public star was beginning to decline. Nonetheless he continued lecturing throughout 1883, except for the short visit to New York for the launch of 'Vera'.

One urgent question that began to concern Oscar was his bachelor status. There can be little doubt that Oscar had a strong attraction to his own sex. His friendships with other men were, if not physical at this point, intellectually passionate to an abnormal degree. In 1883, for instance, he wrote to Robert Sherard:

'As for the dedication of your poems I accept it; how could I refuse a gift so musical in its beauty, and fashioned by one I love so much as I love you? To me the mirror of perfect friendship can never be dulled by any treachery, however mean, or disloyalty, however base.'

The worlds of the theatre and the arts, the two great centres of Oscar's social life, harboured more than their share of pederasts, whilst even the Catholic Church was a haven for many young Victorian males who could not reconcile their sexual inclinations with their moral beliefs. Many of Oscar's literary idols, for instance Whitman and Verlaine, were openly homosexual, whilst his Oxford mentor Walter Pater's circle was noted for its sexual ambivalence. Oscar's critics invariably dismissed his cultural tastes and attitudes as effeminate, and there was some truth in the accusations. Moreover he must have been well aware of the gossip and rumours surrounding him. Yet if Wilde had stood at the gate to the forbidden garden of his homosexuality and peered in, nothing suggests that he entered to pick its flowers until later in his life. All of his known sexual liaisons to this date were with women – here a visit to a brothel in the United States, there a love letter to an unidentified correspondent named Hattie,

'But when I think of America I only remember someone whose lips are like the crimson petals of a summer rose, whose eyes are two brown agates, who has the fascination of a panther, the pluck of a tigress and the grace of a bird. Darling Hattie, I now realize that I am absolutely in love with you, and for ever and ever your devoted friend.'

Marriage was both a desirable and an inevitable step on the ladder of Victorian life, and Oscar had been casting about for a suitable partner since his Oxford days. In 1880, after his failure to win Florence Balcombe, he proposed to Violet Hunt – 'the sweetest violet in England' as he described her. Hunt, a future novelist herself, spurned his offer and later married the American writer Ford Madox Ford. A little later Wilde proposed again, this time to the beautiful heiress Charlotte Montefiore. When she declined he sent her a note which read 'Charlotte, I am so sorry about your decision. With your money and my brains, we could have gone far.' But by 1883, as he approached his thirtieth year, Oscar felt a strong need for the companionship, stability and financial security he hoped wedlock promised. Above all, perhaps, he wanted children to carry his name and fame down to the next generation.

In November 1883 Oscar's lecture tour took him to Dublin, and whilst in the city he made a momentous decision. For several years he had been intermittently meeting a young woman named Constance Lloyd. Over the period the couple had drawn close, and it was clear that she was waiting for him to propose to her. Constance, although not as fantastically rich as a Charlotte Montefiore, had a comfortable income of £250 a year from her rich barrister grandfather, a not inconsiderable sum to the impecunious Oscar. The lawyer approved of the match, and indicated that the couple could expect a sizable dowry on their marriage. In addition to financial considerations Constance was extremely beautiful, and had a good intellect and pleasant disposition. She also idolized her unusual suitor. Shortly after meeting Oscar in 1881 she wrote to her half-brother Otho praising him.

'O.W. came yesterday at 5.30 (by which time I was shaking with fright) and stayed for half an hour, begged me to come and see his mother again soon, which little request I need hardly say I have kept to myself. I can't help liking him, because when he's talking to me alone he's never a bit affected, and speaks naturally, except that he uses better language than most people. Grandpa, I think, likes Oscar, but of course the others laugh at him, because they don't choose to see anything but that he wears long hair and looks aesthetic.'

Constance Mary Lloyd was born in 1858 in Dublin, and spent her early childhood in the city. Her fathe, Horace Lloyd QC, a gifted but somewhat scandalous barrister, died in 1874 leaving very little money to his family. Following the re-marriage of her mother, whom Constance detested because of her bitter temper, the family moved to London. Several times a year, however, she returned to Ireland and visited her grandfather, John Lloyd, to whom she was closer than her mother and stepfather. Constance was a bright, well-educated girl, who could speak several languages and had travelled extensively in Europe. She had spent some of her teenage years lodging at Babbacombe Cliff House with her distant relative Lady Mount Temple, a patron of the pre-Raphaelite painters. With her aesthetic philosophy, dark beauty and lithe, almost boyish, body, the young Irishwoman appeared to be the perfect partner for Oscar.

The slow courtship continued over the next few years, encouraged by Speranza, who liked Constance and decided she would be an ideal daughter-in-law. It took a while for Oscar to come round to his mother's point of view, but with some encouragement he eventually fell in love with Constance. On Sunday 25 November 1883 he proposed to her in the same drawing room where her father had proposed to her mother thirty years previously. 'Prepare yourself for an astounding piece of news,' she wrote to Otho. 'I am engaged to Oscar Wilde, and perfectly and insanely happy.' Oscar, now that he had at last taken the plunge, was equally taken with his fiancée. 'I am going to be married to a beautiful girl called Constance Lloyd,' he informed Lily Langtry, 'a grave, slight, violet-eyed little Artemis, with great coils of heavy brown hair which make her flower-like head droop like a blossom, and wonderful ivory hands which draw music from the piano so sweet that the birds stop singing to listen to her.'

Some biographers have suggested his motives in wishing to marry were entirely cynical, but this is grossly unfair. Oscar was undoubtedly calculating in his choice of a bride, but he did not intend his marriage to be a sham. He was not trying to hide or subvert his homosexuality, but rather had deluded himself that loving Woman's beauty meant that he also loved women. In a marriage, as he was to discover, you cannot hide the reality of your inner nature behind an ideal. In the following years the pressure of his sexual and emotional yearning towards other men, and its inevitable consequences, would lead to unfathomable anguish both for himself and his bride. Oscar's expectations that marital love would resolve any sexual division in his soul were high.

'Love is the sacrament of life,' says the character Guido in Oscar's 'Duchess of Padua'. 'It sets Virtue where virtue was not; Cleanses men of all the vile pollutions of this world.' Equally the Duchess in that play predicts the harsh truth of what the woman Oscar married might expect. 'The love of men turns women into martyrs; for its sake we do and suffer anything.'

Oscar Wilde and Constance Lloyd were married on 28 May 1884 at St James's Church, London, following which they honeymooned in Paris and Dieppe. Constance's grandfather died shortly after the wedding, and she found her annual allowance increased to £900 a year. This was in addition to £5,000 he had already given the couple so that they could purchase the lease of a house in Tite Street, where Wilde had briefly lived with Frank Miles some years previously. The young lovers now made plans to decorate their new home. For Oscar it was an opportunity to put the ideas he preached in 'The House Beautiful' into practice, and he spared no expense on the work. Once again he employed the architect Edwin Godwin, who had designed the earlier house in Tite Street, and with his assistance worked out a décor and colour scheme. The refurbishment took over six months, and was punctuated by endless arguments between Wilde and his contractors, who found it almost impossible to meet the exacting standards he demanded of them. But the premises, when eventually completed, impressed all who came to visit. Wilde eschewed the stifling furnishings and garish pre-Raphaelite-inspired patterned fabrics that were in fashion at the period. His own tastes were subtler and tended towards white walls and pastel colours, with exquisite splashes of colour. The Irish poet W. B. Yeats, who visited the house on a number of occasions, remembered the red shade on a terracotta figurine lamp, that stood on an identically shaded red cloth draped over a snow-white table.

Oscar's son Vivian later described the dining room, where the white walls were matched with white Chippendale chairs and a white carpet. The alpine starkness of the room was relieved by the use of pale blue and yellow trimmings. The genius of Wilde as an interior designer has sadly been lost, since there are no surviving examples of his work, nor even any photographs of the rooms in Tite Street. This is to be regretted, since it was an important facet of his talent, and made him the spiritual precursor of the modern 'style guru'. Oscar was never shy about promoting his views on design, particularly those on the need for more individual taste in clothing, which had become one of his obsessions. Constance found herself paraded around in an array of increasingly bizarre period costumes designed by her husband, all in the name of Dress Reform. In 1887, for instance, she was introduced to Queen Victoria; a spectator noted her costume, 'limp white muslin with no bustle, saffron coloured silk swathed about her shoulders, a huge cartwheel Gainsboro hat, white and bright-yellow stockings and shoes ... she looked too hopeless, and we thought her shy and dull.' In 1884 Oscar added 'A Discourse on Dress' to his list of lectures, along with another on 'The Value of Art in Modern Life'. But his claim that he had 'civilized the provinces' with his lecture tours was hollow. By 1886 Oscar Wilde had ceased to interest the general public. In that year the magazine *Punch*, which had caricatured him in almost every edition during his aesthetic heyday, did not consider him worthy of a single cartoon. Oscar was bored with lecturing, and as his income dwindled, he began to concentrate on more lucrative work.

He found a ready market for his literary skills as a critic for fashionable journals like *The Pall Mall Gazette* and *The Dramatic Review.* His book and drama reviews were like himself, witty, opinionated and sometimes waspish. As a literary critic Oscar was wide-ranging and astute, and often pressed the superiority of the French novel over its less daring English counterpart. He also enjoyed a literary joke, as in the following review in *The Pall Mall Gazette* of 15 February 1888.

' 'The Chronicle of the Mites' is a mock-heroic poem about the inhabitants of a decaying cheese who speculate about the origin of their species and hold learned discussions upon the meaning of evolution and the Gospel according to Darwin. This cheese-epic is a rather unsavoury production and the style is so monstrous and so realistic that the author should be called the Gorgon-Zola of literature.'

In 1886 Oscar Wilde was in his thirty-second year. He was now the proud father of two sons, Cyril and Vivian, born in 1885 and 1886, and appeared to be settling down into an existence that was almost bourgeois in its respectability. It was a façade, for in reality he was dissatisfied with Constance and bored with the constricting ties of marriage. 'You know I am not an admirer of marriage,' Lord Henry states in *Dorian Gray.* 'The real drawback to marriage is that it makes one unselfish. And unselfish people are colourless. They lack individuality.' Oscar, moreover, was becoming all too aware that his true sexual orientation was not towards women. Constance's two pregnancies had changed her boyish, sylph-like figure into that of a mature woman, and it disgusted him. The writer and publisher Frank Harris, in his biography of Oscar, recalls a conversation they had around this time. Wilde spoke of his loathing for Constance's body during her two pregnancies, describing it as 'heavy, shapeless, deformed'. Oscar loved his two sons beyond measure, but now that the first flush of passion had died down, his sexual interest in his wife was declining rapidly. Constance's involvement in bringing up her two young children restricted her social life, and gave Oscar freedom to follow his own pursuits outside the home. Gradually but inexorably the couple began to drift apart.

In the spring of 1887 Wilde was offered a job that would allow him the free time he needed to write for himself. The publishing firm of Cassell and Company had launched a magazine called *The Lady's World* about eight months previously, but it had not been doing very well. They wished to appoint a new editor in an effort to revive the publication, and settled on Oscar as the ideal candidate. His strong views on female emancipation, and his connections with the great actresses and society personalities of London, suggested that he would improve the content of the faltering journal and make it more attractive to its female readers. For a few months Wilde did not disappoint his employers, and threw himself into the editorship. He insisted that the title should be changed to *Woman's World* because 'It seems to me that at present it is too feminine and not sufficiently womanly.' Articles were commissioned from social leaders like the Queen of Romania and Lady Archibald Campbell, and Sarah Bernhardt was persuaded to write about 'The History of My Tea Gown'. Oscar even wrote to Queen Victoria, and sought permission to print a selection of her early poems. The monarch was not amused. 'Really, what will people not say and invent,' she noted in her journal. 'Never could the Queen in her whole life write one line of poetry, serious or comic.'

For a while Oscar dutifully took the London underground railway into the offices of Cassell and Co to oversee the magazine, but following an initial burst of enthusiasm his interest flagged. He began to treat the job as a stipend, with the reluctant collusion of his employers, who appreciated the value of the name Oscar Wilde on the magazine's masthead. 'I used to go three times a week for an hour a day,' he told W. B. Yeats shortly before quitting the job in 1889, 'but I have struck off one of the days.' The editorship, despite Oscar's casual indolence towards it, provided a steady income, and allowed him time to write the short stories and essays that marked his flowering as a creative writer.

The first of his literary efforts to be published was a book of original fairy tales, *The Happy Prince and Other Stories*, which was published in 1888. Oral storytelling is a traditional skill in Ireland, and a repertoire of old tales has been passed down the centuries. Wilde must have inherited this gift from his Irish ancestors, for his talents as a weaver of tales were extraordinary. André Gide, who met Wilde in Paris in 1891, wrote in his memoir *Oscar Wilde* that 'Wilde did not converse; he narrated.' Gide recorded some of the stories that he heard Oscar tell, whose themes and styles share much with some of those in his first volume of fairy tales and its sequel, *The House of Pomegranates*, published in 1891. It has sometimes been suggested that Wilde composed the stories in *The Happy Prince* for his children, but this is an oversimplification. It was rather that fatherhood turned his mind towards the idea of framing and publishing his stories as fairy tales. He was well aware that books of literary fairy stories, often in expensive illustrated editions, were fashionable and extremely popular with Victorian readers. Wilde commissioned two artists to draw the pictures for *The Happy Prince*, Jacomb Hood and the great nineteenth-century illustrator Walter Crane.

Many of Wilde's children's stories were intended to appeal equally to adults. He described them as 'written not for children, but for childlike adults between eighteen and eighty'. They are allegorical or satirical, and reflect Wilde's aesthetic obsession with the importance of Beauty. But perhaps the strongest quality is the sadness that runs through so many of the tales, which sometimes (as in 'The Selfish Giant') appears to reflect his own inner regrets. Often the stories dwell on suffering and redemption. They end in sorrow and death rather than 'And so they lived happily ever after'. 'The Happy Prince', perhaps the most famous of Oscar's children's stories, is typically melancholy. It was first related in 1885, to a group of Oscar's aesthetic Cambridge disciples calling themselves the 'cicadas'. He is believed to have written the tale down shortly afterwards. A swallow falls in love with a reed, and then with the Happy Prince, a statue in the palace of St Souci. The Prince stares out over the city and sees its suffering poor. He asks the swallow to take his ruby sword pommel, his sapphire eyes and his gold leaf to give to the hungry people in the streets below. The swallow wants to fly south to join his flock in Egypt, but stays to help out of love for the statue. At last the bird realizes winter has come, and he is about to die. With his last breath the swallow kisses the Happy Prince and falls dead to the ground; simultaneously the statue's lead heart breaks in two. The people of the town, seeing the statue has lost its jewels and gold leaf, put it in a furnace, but they cannot melt down the pieces of the broken heart. They are thrown away, and God sends an angel to bring the lead heart and the dead sparrow, 'the two most precious things in the city', to his garden.

There are elements in the story, for instance in the swallow's love for the unresponsive and unspeaking reed, which hint at Oscar's unhappiness with Constance. Another story, the 'Remarkable Rocket', is more overtly personal, and was intended to be an attack on the artist Whistler. The two men had first met shortly after Oscar came to London, and kept up a friendship for several years thereafter. Whistler, like Oscar, was a dandy and a wit, with equally pronounced views on art. Their friendly bantering is reflected in the telegrams they sent each other in 1883, when *Punch* published a satirical conversation in which they discussed the English theatre:

> Wilde: *Punch* is too ridiculous. We never talk about any
> thing but ourselves when we are together.
> Whistler: No, No, Oscar. We never talk about anything
> but me.
> Oscar: It is true, Jimmy, we were talking about you, but I
> was thinking about myself.

On Oscar's wedding day Whistler sent Oscar another telegram: 'Fear I might not be able to reach you in time. Don't wait.'

Whistler was notorious for his vanity, and usually ended up by falling out with his friends over one issue or another.

In 1884 Wilde lectured at the Royal Academy of Art, and the artist was annoyed to find that Oscar had plagiarized many of his ideas. He gave vent to his anger at the reception held afterwards. During their conversation Whistler said, 'You must never say a painting is good or bad. You may say "I like this", or "I do not like that".' Wilde was impressed with the epigram and commented 'I wish I had said that.' Whistler's famous reply was, 'You will, Oscar, you will.' Afterward he became increasingly hostile to his former friend, bombarding him with slighting letters and personal insults. Wilde was stung, and retaliated by mocking the artist as 'The Remarkable Rocket', who makes statements like 'In fact you should be thinking about me. I am always thinking about myself and I expect others to do the same', or 'The only thing that sustains one through life is the consciousness of the immense inferiority of everybody else, and this is a feeling I have always cultivated.'

Oscar did not limit himself to writing for children, and submitted a number of adult stories to the popular magazines. 'The Model Millionaire' and 'The Sphinx without a Secret' were very slight pieces, and obviously churned out to make a quick profit. But 'The Canterville Ghost', first published in 1886, was a charming parody of the Gothic horror story. This comic tale of the supernatural concerns the feud between the resident ghost of an English castle and a pushy family of American tenants, who refuse to be frightened off by his haunting. The ending of 'The Canterville Ghost', despite the story's generally broad humour, returns to Wilde's favourite theme of the redemption of evil through love. The ghost is only freed from the penalty of its crimes when the innocent daughter of the house prays for him, and weeps for his sorrow. Oscar hoped to make a financial killing by selling the story in the United States, but the plan backfired. A year later he was writing to the *New York Tribune*, which had published the piece without acknowledging the author or paying for it.

Wilde, as the 1880s drew towards a close, was beginning to make a living from his writing. He had almost entirely ceased to give public lectures, and was phasing out his reviewing and journalistic activities. But just as Oscar established his literary credentials, he entered on a new phase in his private life. At last he began to throw off the cloak of self-deception that concealed his true sexual orientation. The path ahead wrecked his marriage, and would eventually destroy him as a public figure, but his liberation sparked the sustained burst of creative energy that produced his greatest fiction and drama.

CHAPTER VI

THE MAN OF MASKS

Literary success added a new sheen to Oscar's reputation as a lecturer, journalist and wit. He had grown from the flashy young aesthete of his earlier years into a self-possessed and powerful presence, who dominated those around him by the strength of his personality. There was an arrogant quality in his pronouncements, relieved only by his humour and that marvellous power to conjure up almost hypnotic fables at the drop of a hat. Oscar had many friends in London society, but there were others who considered him a disturbing and even dangerous influence. His critics pointed to the circle of young men in whose company he was often seen, and speculated about his relationship with them. Were it not for Wilde's happy marriage, his beautiful wife and two fine sons, there might have been many more questions about his sexuality.

In fact Oscar's apparent marital happiness had become a mask by 1890, behind which he hid his secret homosexual life. It was inevitable that sooner or later this part of his personality must fulfil itself. The real question is why it took so many years for Wilde to accept the reality that his heterosexuality was false. In 1886, on a visit to Oxford, Oscar met Robert Ross, a seventeen-year old scholar who was preparing to sit exams for Cambridge University. Ross was a Canadian by birth, but had spent most of his life in England, where he embraced the aesthetic philosophy. He was overtly homosexual, and made it clear he was attracted to Oscar, who described him as having 'the face of a Puck'. The older man was flattered, and on the evening before his birthday in October had his first known sexual encounter with a male lover. The experience proved an irrevocable turning point. Robbie Ross moved into the Wilde house as a paying guest, and for three months Oscar carried on an affair with his teenage lover almost in front of his unsuspecting wife. After his initial physical relationship with Ross ended, Wilde began to explore his own sexuality, and soon attracted a circle of young male admirers. Robert Ross remained a close friend, and for the rest of Oscar's life could be counted on as one of his most reliable companions. He was Wilde's trusted confidant through all that was to come, and showed great loyalty during his mentor's public disgrace and imprisonment. Ross was beside Oscar's bed during his last fatal sickness in Paris, and afterwards acted as his literary executor.

Oscar's homosexual activities dealt an irreparable blow to his faltering marriage to Constance. He had no desire to leave his wife, if for no other reason than the sake of his children. Nor did he wish to cut off his daily communications with his family or move out of the Tite Street house. His attitude towards Constance at this period is suggested by a passage in his novel *Dorian Gray*. 'The only way a woman can reform a man is by boring him so completely that he loses all possible interest in life. If you had married this girl you would have been wretched. Of course you would have treated her kindly. One can always be kind to people about whom one cares nothing.' Oscar stopped having physical relations with his wife after meeting Ross, probably using the excuse that the syphilis of his Oxford years had recurred. Henceforth they would be friends and domestic partners, but that was all. Constance Wilde's apparent ignorance of her husband's homosexuality remains something of a mystery. Some of Oscar's biographers have mistaken her shyness in public for stupidity, but this is unfair. Constance had a determined personality, and actively pursued her interests in women's suffrage and the Theosophical movement. She also made time in her busy social and domestic schedule to write two children's books. The key to Constance's wilful ignorance of her husband's secret life lies in her own troubled childhood rather than any lack of sensitivity. Her father's notorious gambling and drinking habits had left the Lloyd family with a horror of scandal. Oscar's wife was determined that her sons would be spared the shame and domestic quarrels that had blighted her own childhood. To keep the illusion of domestic respectability she swallowed her rejection and jealousy, and accepted the pretence that her husband's male friends were simply his disciples. She became like the three monkeys in Kipling's story, who could hear no evil, see no evil and speak no evil.

Wilde was a man of masks, and could present different faces to his London acquaintances, his wife, and his circle of young admirers. The duality between the façade of a dutiful husband and the other, 'sinful' life he secretly led, attracted him like a magnet. As early as 1884, for example, he had written to a Cambridge friend, 'I would sacrifice everything for a new experience and know there is no such thing as a new experience at all ... I would go the stake and be a skeptic to the last ... There is an unknown land full of strange flowers and subtle perfumes, a land of which it is a joy of all joys to dream, a land where all things are perfect and poisonous.' The widespread prejudice against homosexuality in England gave Oscar additional reason to be circumspect. In 1885 the Criminal Amendment Act made sexual acts between men illegal under English law, with severe penalties including long terms of imprisonment. The Cleveland Street Scandal of 1889 was an advance warning of what he might expect if arrested on indecency charges by the police. In that year Lord Arthur Somerset was forced to flee England after being apprehended at a male brothel, where clients were serviced by 'telegraph boys'. He was not the only public figure to frequent the premises, but an official cover-up protected the other distinguished clients involved. Physical assaults on suspected homosexuals were also common. In 1889, for instance, Robert Ross was thrown in a fountain by fellow Cambridge undergraduates who disapproved of his long hair and aesthetic manners. The prank went sour when he came down with pneumonia and almost died, but the main instigator of the attack went unpunished.

Oscar, then, had strong reasons for exercising some discretion in his public behaviour. To the friends outside his inner circle he was the same bright spirit that he had always been, the conversationalist and wit whose warm smile could light up a room. One of Wilde's finest traits was his kindness to younger writers. Whilst he might sometimes be a harsh critic of his literary peers, he was quick to recognize new talent and encourage it. Amongst those who benefited from his interest was the great Irish poet W. B. Yeats. In his autobiography *The Trembling of the Veil* he recorded his impressions of Wilde, whom he first met in 1887 or 1888. Oscar, believing that the young Irishman was alone in London, invited him to Christmas dinner at his Tite Street house. The poet was astounded by Oscar's ability to speak in perfect sentences, and thought that even the most casual utterances sounded as if they had been written on the previous night. In retrospect Yeats felt that the late 1880s were the happiest years of Oscar's life, and stated: 'he seemed to live in the enjoyment of his own spontaneity'. Yet the young Irish poet sensed the falsity in his fellow-countryman's public face, as if the House Beautiful was part of an imaginary life, and his relentless pursuit of the English aristocracy a play in which he was Jack climbing a pantomime Beanstalk. Yeats, who knew the history of the Wilde family, believed his host had created this illusory perfection as a reaction to the disordered atmosphere of his own childhood.

In his autobiography, Yeats quoted Oscar's opinion of another renowned Anglo-Irish writer. 'Mr Bernard Shaw has no enemies but is intensely disliked by all his friends,' the poet heard him say. Shaw began to establish his literary name around 1885, as the music critic of the *Star* newspaper. Oscar sympathized with Shaw's socialist beliefs, and in May 1886 signed a petition organized by the journalist to support the organizers of the Haymarket Riots in Chicago. Shaw was grateful, especially since he had previously considered Oscar a snob, and the two men kept up their casual acquaintance. In 1893, after the English production of 'Salome' was banned, Oscar sent a copy of the published edition of the play to Shaw, with a note thanking him for his support in the controversy. 'My dear Shaw, you have written well and wisely and with sound wit on the ridiculous institution of stage censorship; your little book on Ibsenism and Ibsen is such a delight to me that I constantly take it up, and always find it stimulating and refreshing; England is the land of intellectual fog but you have done much to clear the air; we are both Celtic and I like to think we are friends.' In 1898, after his release from prison, Wilde included Shaw on the list of friends and reviewers to receive complimentary copies of the limited edition of 'The Ballad of Reading Gaol'.

In 1889 Wilde published three works that expounded his philosophy on the relationship between art and life. Two of these were essays, a literary form in which he excelled. 'Pen, Pencil and Poison' was an account of the life and crimes of Thomas Wainewright, the early nineteenth-century essayist and poet who was also a notorious forger and mass murderer. Wainewright, who is believed to have poisoned at least four people, was eventually convicted and transported to Tasmania, where he died in 1852. Wilde's essay, which was first published by Frank Harris in the *Fortnightly Review* of January 1889, explored the relationship between his subject's crimes and his talents as a writer. Oscar portrays Wainewright as a Renaissance man born out of his time, and argues that his crimes were an integral part of his genius.

'The fact of a man being a poisoner is nothing against his prose. The domestic virtues are not the true basis of art, although they may serve as an excellent advertisement for second-rate artists ... That he (Wainewright) had a sincere love of art and nature seems to me quite certain. There is no essential incongruity between crime and culture. We cannot rewrite the whole of history for the purpose of gratifying our moral sense of what should be.'

'The Decay of Lying' – first published in *Nineteenth Century* magazine in the same month as 'Pen, Pencil and Poison' – is one of Oscar's best essays. Its theme that art creates life, rather than the other way round, was the essence of Wilde's own philosophy. 'Paradox though it may seem – and paradoxes are always dangerous things – it is none the less true that life imitates art far more than art imitates life.' After condemning the trend towards realism in modern literature – 'the modern novelist presents us with dull facts in the form of fiction' – Oscar presents his case 'that lying, the telling of beautiful untrue things, is the proper aim of art'. He argues that the artist's duty is to make illusions and masks, and reiterates his belief that 'art never expresses anything but itself'. In his view 'Life holds the mirror up to Art, and either reproduces some strange type imagined by painter or sculptor, or realizes in fact what has been dreamed in fiction.' 'The Decay of Lying' was framed as a Platonic dialogue between friends, a form of philosophical essay familiar to Wilde from his study of Greek at Trinity and Oxford. To an extent this mirrored the origins of the piece, which Oscar was inspired to write following a conversation with Robert Ross.

Another discussion with Ross provided the basis of the short story 'The Portrait of Mr W. H.', certainly the most sophisticated of Oscar's stories, and without doubt the best. The narrative's subtle mixing of fiction with fact illustrates many of the principles laid down in 'The Decay of Lying'. The story has the quality of a lie chasing a dream. A nameless narrator, presumably Wilde himself, hears about the portrait from an acquaintance named Erskine. 'Mr W. H.' is a reference to the unknown person to whom Shakespeare dedicated his sonnets. Erskine tells the narrator about the scholar

Cyril Grahame, and his theory, evolved through a close study of the sonnets, that Mr W. H. was Will Hughes, an Elizabethan boy actor off whom Shakespeare was enamoured. Grahame, unable to discover proof that such a person ever existed, commissions a forged portrait of the actor, and pretends to find it attached to the side of an old Elizabethan chest he purchases. Erskine is taken in at first, but afterwards accidentally discovers the forgery. He confronts Cyril Grahame with his dishonesty, and the disgraced scholar shoots himself. The narrator finds himself believing Grahame's theory, and urges Erskine to continue the quest for documents that will confirm the existence of Will Hughes. But on reflection he realizes that the actor is a figment of Grahame's imagination, and begs Erskine to disregard his advice. He is too late, for the man has become obsessed with proving that there was a Will Hughes in Shakespeare's theatre company. Two years later Erskine writes to tell the narrator he has failed to find any historical records mentioning the actor. He has lost faith in the theory, and now intends to kill himself. The narrator is horrified to hear that his acquaintance has indeed died, and hurries off to give his condolences to his family. To his surprise he discovers the cause of death was not suicide but consumption. Erskine bequeaths the forged portrait to the narrator, who hangs it in his library and passes it off as a genuine painting of Will Hughes.

'The Portrait of Mr W. H.' prefigures the world-famous short stories of the Argentinean writer, Jorge Luis Borges, a great admirer of Wilde's literary works. Its assumption that Shakespeare was homosexual, although toned down in the version published by *Blackwood's* magazine in 1889, added extra fuel to rumours about the author's own sexuality. The story had a curious sequel, when Wilde commissioned a fashionable London artist, Charles Ricketts, to paint the mythical Will Hughes in the style of the French master Clouet. He was enthralled with Rickett's work, which was hung in the library of his house in Tite Street. The painting was sold along with Wilde's other possessions in 1895, and has sadly since vanished without a trace.

Charles Ricketts and his associate Charles Shannon were book illustrators, with whom Oscar afterwards formed a close professional association. They were appointed 'official artists to Oscar Wilde', and from 1889 onwards designed all his books except the published edition of the play 'Salome', which utilized Aubrey Beardsley's famous drawings. The artists were part of an exceptional coterie of talented young men who surrounded Oscar at the height of his fame. Some were writers like the poet Richard le Gallienne and the novelist André Raffalovich; the latter included pen portraits of Oscar and Constance in his novel *A Willing Exile*, under the names of Cyprian and Daisy Brome. Amongst Oscar's closest friends was the poet John Gray, who is often put forward as the original model for the fictional Dorian Gray. The exquisitely handsome Gray, the son of a carpenter, was Oscars principal romantic interest between 1889 and the arrival on the scene of Lord Alfred Douglas in 1892. Another of Oscar's disciples was Max Beerbohm, the younger brother of the actor and theatrical impresario Herbert Beerbohm Tree. Max Beerbohm was still at school when he first met Oscar in 1888. He admired the older man's intellect but did not share his sexual tastes, and later turned against him. Oscar recognized the youngster's exceptional promise, and commented that 'He plays with words as one plays with what one loves.' Beerbohm emerged as the most successful of the writers and artists in Wilde's London circle, and later achieved fame with novels like *Zuleika Dobson*, his short stories and his cartoons.

A number of Wilde's friends were undergraduates he had met on his regular visits to Oxford University. One of the oddest was John Barlas, a half-crazed religious maniac who was arrested for plotting to blow up the Houses of Parliament. The episode led to Oscar saying 'when I think of the harm the Bible has done I am quite ashamed of it'. In 1890 Oscar was introduced to an exceptionally promising poet named Lionel Johnson, at that time studying at New College. The friendship turned to bitter enmity in 1892, when Wilde began his scandalous relationship with Johnson's cousin, Lord Alfred Douglas. The enraged young poet wrote a sonnet attacking Wilde as 'The Destroyer of Souls', whilst Oscar said of his slightly built critic: 'Every morning at 11 o'clock you can see him come out of the Café Royal and hail the first passing perambulator.'

Not all of Wilde's social activities revolved around his circle of aspiring young writers and artists. He was equally at ease with powerful political leaders like Charles Stuart Parnell, the Anglo-Irish landlord who led the Home Rule party in the House of Commons. In 1887 the London *Times* published the forged Piggott letters, which accused Parnell of complicity in the Phoenix Park murders and other acts of terrorism. Oscar and his journalist brother Willie strongly supported Parnell during the controversy that followed, and attended the sessions of the Parliamentary Commission that cleared the Irish leader. Shortly afterwards Parnell's political reputation was shattered when he was cited in the Kitty

O'Shea divorce case. He spent the last two years of his life in a desperate effort to keep control of the Irish party, and died exhausted at Brighton in October 1891. Wilde followed Parnell's decline with sadness. 'The greatest men fail, or seem to have failed' was his final comment on the leader who came within a hairsbreadth of securing Irish independence.

In 1888 Oscar began working on his only novel, *The Picture of Dorian Gray*. In September of that year the American publisher J. M. Stoddart arrived in England looking for contributors to the periodical *Lippincott's Monthly Magazine*. He arranged a meeting with Oscar and Arthur Conan Doyle, the author of the immensely successful Sherlock Holmes stories. Both men agreed to submit long works, Doyle his second Holmes novel *The Sign of Four* and Wilde *The Picture of Dorian Gray*. Oscar did not have his book written in time for its deadline, and was unable to deliver it until the spring of 1889. It first appeared in *Lippincott's Monthly* in June 1890, and was published in book form in the following year.

As a novel *Dorian Gray* has many faults, but it uniquely reflects the character and interests of its author. Wilde's aestheticism, his attraction to the supernatural, his conversation, and his homosexuality – all are represented in *Dorian Gray*. Whilst it is not his masterpiece – that plaudit must go to 'The Importance of Being Earnest' – the novel has a personal relevance that his plays lack. The theme reflects Oscar's obsession with the masks behind which we hide the true reality of our souls. Dorian Gray, the handsome protagonist of the story, is painted by the artist Basil Hallward, who has become infatuated by him. But Dorian is influenced by a book he is given by the cynical Lord Henry Wotton, a friend of Hallward's. After he provokes the suicide of his fiancée, the actress Sibyl Vane, Dorian discovers that the portrait is beginning to age, and hides it in his attic. Dorian's appearance defies time as the years pass, and he stays a beautiful young man, but his evil actions take their toll on the face of the portrait, which grows hideous as it ages. At length Dorian shows Basil Hallward the painting, and then murders the artist and persuades a friend (who later commits suicide) to dispose of the body with chemicals. He is responsible for the accidental death of the brother of Sibyl Vane, who recognizes his sister's nemesis in one of the low dens he frequents. But as he enters middle-age, Dorian grows weary of his life of vice, and falls in love with a young woman named Hetty Merton. He attempts to destroy the foul portrait by stabbing it with the same knife he used to kill Hallward, in the belief that this will cleanse his polluted soul. The servants hear a scream, and rushing upstairs find the body of a loathsome old man lying on the floor, and a splendid portrait of their master hanging on the wall.

Many books influenced the plot of *Dorian Gray*, ranging from the author's own great-uncle's classic Gothic novel *Melmoth the Wanderer* to Disraeli's *Vivian Grey*. But Oscar's most important example was probably Robert Louis Stevenson's supernatural horror story, *Dr Jekyll and Mr Hyde*, which had enjoyed huge success on its publication some years previously. Wilde, however, used his story to promote his theories about art and decadence. The decadent atmosphere of *Dorian Gray* owed much to the novel *A Rebours*, by the French writer Joris-Karl Huysmans, which profoundly affected Wilde when he first read it on his honeymoon with Constance in 1884. *A Rebours* is the 'yellow book' that first opens Dorian Gray's eyes to the world of the senses:

'It was the strangest book he had ever read ... It was a novel without a plot, and with only one character, being indeed, simply a psychological study of a certain young Parisian, who spent his life trying to realize in the nineteenth century all the passions and modes of thought that belonged to every century except his own ... One hardly knew at times whether one was reading the spiritual ecstasies of a medieval saint or the morbid confessions of a modern sinner. It was a poisonous book.'

Dorian's sins remain nameless in the novel, but the ambivalence of his relationship with his own sex is obvious. 'Why is your friendship so fatal to young men?' Basil Hallward asks him in one passage.

'There was that wretched boy in the Guards who committed suicide ... you were his great friend. There was Sir Henry Ashton, who had to leave England, with a tarnished name. You and he were inseparable. What about Adrian Singleton and his dreadful end? What about Lord Kent's son, and his career? I met his father yesterday in St James's Street. He seemed broken with shame and sorrow. What about the young Duke of Perth? What sort of life has he got now? What gentlemen would associate with him?'

Oscar saw much of himself in Dorian and the other major characters in the book. 'Basil Hallward is what I think I am,' he said, 'Lord Henry is what the world thinks me. Dorian is what I would like to be – in other ages perhaps.' Yet his true fictional alter ego is the witty and cynical Lord Henry Wotton, who acts as a mouthpiece for the author's views on Art,

Beauty and Society. Although the Victorian public were offended by the decadent atmosphere of *Dorian Gray*, modern readers might take more umbrage at Lord Henry's masculine chauvinism, as in this example:

'I am afraid that women appreciate cruelty, downright cruelty, more than anything else. They have wonderfully primitive instincts. We have emancipated them, but they remain slaves looking for their masters just the same. They love being dominated.'

The Picture of Dorian Gray met a storm of criticism from reviewers and public alike on its publication in *Lippincott's Monthly*, often directed at the author as much as the book. Constance was heard to remark 'Since Oscar wrote *Dorian Gray* nobody will talk to us any more.' Some of the abuse was not altogether disinterested. Charles Whibley of the *Scots Observer*, for instance, was a close friend and future brother-in-law of Wilde's bitter rival, Whistler. His review of *Dorian Gray* accused its author of 'grubbing about in muck heaps', and included an insulting reference to the Clarendon Street Scandal: 'But if he can write for none but outlawed noblemen and perverted telegraph boys, the sooner he can take to tailoring (or some other decent trade) the better for his own reputation and the public morals.' Oscar responded with a letter refuting the allegation that the novel reflected his own private life and personal beliefs:

'Your critic then, sir, commits the absolutely unpardonable crime of trying to confuse the artist with his subject matter. For this, sir, there is no excuse at all. One stands remote from one's subject matter. One creates it, and one contemplates it. The further away the subject matter is, the more freely can the artist work. Your reviewer suggests that I do not make it sufficiently clear whether I prefer virtue to wickedness, or wickedness to virtue. An artist, sir, has no ethical sympathies at all. Virtue and wickedness are to him simply what the colours on his palette are to the painter. They are no more and they are no less. He sees that by their means a certain artistic effect can be produced, and he produces it.'

The Picture of Dorian Gray was a commercial success despite the controversy surrounding it, and today ranks with *Frankenstein* and *Dr Jekyll and Mr Hyde* as one of the classic English novels of the supernatural. The book brought its author fame, notoriety and money in equal portions, but if the truth were told his literary future did not lie with the novel or the short story. The epigrams that studded the pages of *Dorian Gray* hinted at the new direction Wilde's writing was about to take. In 1892 Oscar would return to the theatre, where his sparkling dialogue enthralled London audiences in the finest comedies of the nineteenth century.

CHAPTER VII

RETURN TO THE THEATRE

The year 1891 saw Wilde at the height of his creative powers. His apparent indolence was an illusion behind which he worked prodigiously, writing as fluidly as he talked. Oscar published four books in those twelve months alone, including *Lord Arthur Savile's Crime and Other Stories* and the essays 'The Soul of Man Under Socialism' and 'The Critic As Artist'. More importantly for his future career he wrote two new plays, including his first stage comedy. If *Dorian Gray* had made Oscar notorious, this would make him the most popular dramatist in England.

The genesis of Wilde's return to the theatre may be traced back to late 1890, when George Alexander, the new manager of the St James's Theatre, asked him for a play. At first Oscar offered him 'The Duchess of Padua', but Alexander declined because he thought it would cost too much to produce. Instead he asked for a play with a modern setting, and in February 1891 came forward with an advance of £50. Oscar did not settle down to write the play until the late summer of 1891, after a visit to Lake Windermere in the Lake District. He finished the play, which he titled 'Lady Windermere's Fan', in October and brought it to Alexander. The impresario was so impressed that he offered Oscar £1,000 on the spot. Wilde refused, and instead demanded a percentage of the door receipts. It was a wise choice, from which he would earn £7,000 within a few years. Alexander scheduled 'Lady Windermere's Fan' to open at his theatre in early 1892.

'Salome', the second play Wilde wrote in 1891, owed much to his interest in French literature. In February of that year he again visited Paris, where he met the great Symbolist poet, Stéphane Mallarmé, and the young novelists, André Gide and Pierre Louys. Despite the hostility of Whistler, a close friend of the poet, Oscar was welcomed at the 'mardis' where Mallarmé held court to his circle of admirers. The Frenchman, whose poetry shared the philosophies of art put forward in 'The Decay of Lying' and *Dorian Gray,* deeply impressed him. Oscar decided to write a play in the French language that would epitomize the Symbolist style, an idea he had been considering for several years.

His choice of subject was the Biblical story of Salome, who danced before King Herod, and then demanded the head of John the Baptist as her reward. The theme had inspired Mallarmé's unfinished masterpiece 'Herodiade', and was well known to Wilde through his extensive reading of European literature. The nineteenth-century writers Heine, Flaubert and Laforgue used it as the basis for major literary works, whilst a chapter of Huysman's *ARebours* is devoted to a discussion of Gustave Moreau's two famous paintings of Salome. The exotic and sensual elements in the story of Salome rendered it ideal for the daring play Oscar intended to write. In October 1891 he returned to Paris, where he showed extracts of the half-finished play to Gide and other young French writers. 'Salome' was completed at Babbacombe Cliff near Torquay, the home of Constance's distant relative Lady Mount Temple. The actress Sarah Bernhardt agreed to take the leading role in a London production of the play in the spring of 1892.

Oscar's creative power at this time was parallelled by the almost demonic influence he could exercise on the young men he came in contact with. One of those most deeply affected was André Gide, at that time only beginning the career that would make him one of France's greatest modern writers. Wilde set out to make his new acquaintance question his strict religious and moral Protestant upbringing. The highly strung Gide was emotionally crushed by the older man's paradoxes and strange religious parables, which twisted the orthodox interpretations of the Gospels and Christianity. He grew obsessed with Wilde, and almost suffered a nervous breakdown as a result. Gide found himself spiritually devastated after Oscar left Paris to return to London, and only regained his stability after a period of intense prayer. On 1 January 1892 he wrote 'Wilde did me nothing but harm I believe ...', but he was to meet Oscar again, and would eventually publish his recollections of the Irishman.

In June 1891 the poet Lionel Johnson arrived at Oscar's house in Tite Street with his cousin, Lord Alfred Douglas. The young aristocrat, an aspiring poet, was a great admirer of Wilde's writings and wished to meet his idol. Oscar was enchanted by the boy's exquisite good looks, and gave him a limited edition copy of *Dorian Gray*. On learning that Douglas was studying at Magdalen, his own Oxford college, Wilde offered to come up and coach him for his exams. This casual exchange of pleasantries inaugurated the most significant relationship of Oscar's adult life, a love affair that would eventually lead him to disgrace and the dock of the Old Bailey.

Lord Alfred Douglas was born on 22 October 1870, the third son of the Marquess of Queensberry. His noble Scottish family was one of the most famous in Britain, and included such historical personages as James, the 'Black Douglas', the fourteenth-century earl who ruled Scotland in all but name. It was also known for a hereditary streak of madness that produced monsters like the third Marquess of Queensberry – alleged to have roasted one of his servants over an open fire – and the rakish fourth Earl, 'Old Q', described by a London contemporary as 'a polished sin-worn fragment … ogling and hobbling down St James's Street'. By the latter part of the nineteenth century the Queensberry family were more widely known for their interest in prize fighting and horse racing, but they retained a rather unpleasant reputation. Beneath his outward charm Alfred, or Bosie as he was usually known, could be as reckless and unstable as his ancestors. His friends soon learnt that he was demanding and cruelly selfish, particularly when he did not get his own way.

Many of Bosie's worst qualities could be attributed to his unhappy relationship with his father. John Sholto, the ninth Marquess of Queensberry, represented a type of aristocrat that had been common in Georgian and Regency England, but was an anachronism by the end of the nineteenth century. Born in 1844, he had succeeded to the title at the age of fourteen, after his father's probable suicide. Queensberry was deeply interested in prize fighting, and introduced the rules that today govern boxing. Other than that he had achieved little in his life, and was known mainly for his eccentric behaviour. Queensberry's aggressive promotion of his extreme atheistic beliefs resulted in his being barred from the House of Lords, and he was constantly embroiled in lawsuits and other public controversies. In 1882, for instance, he interrupted a performance of the poet Tennyson's play 'The Promise of May' to complain loudly that it insulted freethinkers. The Marquess was equally unstable in his private life. In 1887 Lady Queensberry, worn out by her husband's sexual indiscretions, fled the family home and instituted divorce proceedings. Her three sons took her side during the scandal that followed, putting further strain on their already unhappy dealings with their bullying father. Bosie was distraught, since he was his mother's favourite child, and took on the role of her protector from Queensberry's wrath. Nevertheless his feelings towards his father were ambivalent. In Bosie's autobiography, whilst commenting that his father's dogs received more attention than his children, he admitted that he admired and even loved the man. In many ways, indeed, his obsessively self-centred personality mirrored that of the stubborn, intractable Marquess. Bosie's fraught relationship with his overbearing father was an unending cycle of bitter feud and occasional reconciliation. It dominated the young man's thoughts and actions, and left him emotionally unstable.

Oscar's love affair with Bosie did not commence until the spring of 1892, when the Oxford student found himself involved with blackmailers after writing an indiscreet letter to another man. He appealed for help to Oscar, who arranged to pay off the criminals through his solicitor George Lewis. During their meetings Wilde formed a deep attraction to the blond-haired aristocrat, and in the early summer Bosie replaced John Gray in his affections. In October of 1892 Oscar and Constance were invited to Bracknell House, the home of Bosie's mother; by the end of the year he and Douglas were inseparable. Bosie made little attempt to conceal that the bond was sexual as well as intellectual, and wrote poems like 'The Two Loves', with its line 'I am the love that dare not speak its name'. He paraded his intimacy with Oscar in front of Robbie Ross and the other men in the author's circle of acolytes. Oscar soon discovered that Bosie, despite his young age, was promiscuous, and had numerous contacts with rent boys and their procurers.

'That you were "very young" when our friendship began?' he wrote to Douglas in 'De Profundis'. 'Your defect was not that you knew so little about life, but that you knew so much. The morning joy of boyhood with its delicate bloom, its clear pure light, its joy of innocence and expectation you had left far behind. With very swift and running feet you had passed from Romance to Realism. The gutter and the things that live in it had begun to fascinate you.'

Oscar, despite his later bitterness, was fascinated by this dark and sensual world, and willingly let himself be drawn into its enticing clutches. In late 1892 he was introduced to Alfred Taylor, a procurer with a stable of youthful male prostitutes. These were invariably working class boys from poor backgrounds, who were willing to provide their services for a good dinner and a couple of pounds. Oscar became close to a number of rent boys, either met through Taylor or passed on by Bosie. Most of them would later testify against him in court. Although Oscar was a generous client, and had a friendly relationship with the young men, blackmail was a constant threat. The danger of using the 'renters' was a major part of their attraction to him, as he explained in 'De Profundis':

'People thought it dreadful of me to have entertained at dinner the evil things of life, and to have found pleasure in their company. But they, from the point of view from which I, as an artist in life approached them, were delightfully suggestive and stimulating. It was like feasting with panthers. The danger was half the excitement ... they were to me the brightest of gilded snakes. Their poison was part of their perfection.'

The money to pay the rent boys, along with the expensive tastes of Bosie, proved a major drain on Oscar's finances. But the success of his plays was making him a wealthy man. 'Lady Windermere's Fan' opened at the St James's Theatre on 20 February 1892. The author's fame guaranteed that the auditorium would be packed by the most fashionable figures from society and the arts. Wilde tried his best not to disappoint them, and attempted to persuade as many of his friends as possible to wear green carnations to the opening night. 'I want a lot of men to wear them, it will annoy the public,' he said. In fact nobody seems to have noticed his small publicity stunt, but he made up for it when he came on stage at the end of the play smoking a cigarette. 'Ladies and gentlemen,' he began, 'I have enjoyed this evening immensely. The actors have given us a charming rendition of a delightful play, and your appreciation has been most intelligent. I congratulate you on the great success of your performance, which persuades me that you think almost as highly of the play as I do myself.' His casual demeanour and comments were appreciated by the audience, but annoyed the drama critics, who generally gave 'Lady Windermere's Fan' bad reviews. Their disapproval had no effect on the play's huge popularity with the theatre-going public. 'I am told that royalty is turned away nightly,' Oscar replied when somebody stopped him on the street to ask how his play was doing. He had good reason to be pleased. Not only was his reputation as a dramatist secured, but his share of the play's profits ensured financial stability into the foreseeable future.

'Lady Windermere's Fan' placed its author firmly in the tradition of such Irish playwrights as Farquhar, Goldsmith and Sheridan, whose comedies had enthralled London audiences during the eighteenth century. Oscar originally intended calling his drama 'A Good Woman', but changed the title on the advice of Lady Jane Wilde. 'It is mawkish. Nobody cares for a good woman,' she wrote to him, '"A Noble Woman" would be better.' Instead he named it after the item on which the denouement of the plot hinges. The 'good woman' is Mrs Erlynne, paradoxically an adventuress in the eyes of society. Although it is not revealed until near the end of the second act, she is the mother of the beautiful and snobbish Lady Windermere, who thinks that she is an orphan. The story begins on the morning of Lady Windermere's twenty-first birthday, for which her husband has presented her with a new fan. Then she discovers that her husband has been giving Mrs Erlynne money, and mistakenly assumes they are lovers. Lady Windermere confronts him, but he claims he feels sorry for the woman, and is trying to help re-establish her social position. When Windermere informs his wife that he has invited Mrs Erlynne to the reception at their house that evening, she threatens to hit her rival with the fan if she comes. Mrs Erlynne arrives at the house that evening, but Lady Windermere is so confused that she drops the fan before she can carry out her threat. Later the wicked Lord Darlington (who also believes Mrs Erlynne is Windermere's mistress) takes advantage of Lady Windermere's distress to invite her to his rooms. She refuses angrily, but then overhears Mrs Erlynne tell Windermere that she is about to marry, and wishes him to give her £2,500 a year. The horrified Lady Windermere at once hurries off to Lord Darlington's rooms, leaving behind a scribbled note for her husband.

The note is discovered by Mrs Erlynne, who follows her daughter to Darlington's rooms. She burns the letter and tells Lady Windermere she is not her husband's mistress. At first the younger woman will not believe her, but Mrs Erlynne begs her to remember her child and she agrees to leave. At that moment Lord Darlington comes home, accompanied by Windermere and some other friends. Mrs Erlynne hides Lady Windermere behind a curtain and slips next door. The men enter and one of them notices the fan, which Windermere recognizes as his wife's. He is horrified and begins to search the room. Before he can find his wife Mrs Erlynne enters, and explains she must have picked up the fan by mistake at the reception. Darlington and Windermere are distracted, allowing Lady Windermere to slip away unseen. In the play's final act Lord and Lady Windermere are reconciled, although neither knows the other's secret. Mrs Erlynne arrives with her fiancé, and announces she has decided to marry and leave the country. She privately tells the husband not to reveal her as Lady Windermere's mother, and before departing asks if she might keep the fan as a souvenir.

The play is full of witty epigrams and comments. Many of the best lines are given to cynical Lord Darlington, such as the famous Wildean witticisms 'I can resist everything, except temptation', 'A cynic is a man who knows the price of everything and the value of nothing' and 'I think that life is far too important a thing ever to talk seriously about it'. Other memorable quotes from the play include 'Nothing looks so like innocence as an indiscretion', 'Experience is the name everyone gives to their mistakes', and 'Men become old, but they never become good'.

Wilde's reaction to his new fame as a dramatist was ambivalent. His remark that 'Lady Windermere's Fan' was 'one of those modern drawing room plays with pink lampshades' disparaged both its quality and intent. Beneath the comedy of its polished verbal surface the play portrayed a heartless and amoral society, where human relations are built on lies and deceit. Whilst many of the characters are sympathetic, they are rarely what they appear to be. The 'bad' Mrs Erlynne behaves heroically, whilst the prim Lady Windermere treats her mother abysmally, and comes close to destroying her marriage out of spite. Even Lord Darlington is not the villain he at first appears; rather he acts as a commentator on the pretensions and hypocrisy of the English aristocracy. Even at his lightest, as in 'Lady Windermere's Fan' and the comedies that followed, Wilde's obsession with paradoxes and masks gave an unexpected social depth to his improbable plots.

Oscar nevertheless viewed his popular plays as of less artistic value than his poetry and the drama 'Salome'. In a sense they financed his lavish lifestyle, but did not fulfill his creative drives. Whilst the success of 'Lady Windermere's Fan' was gratifying, Wilde's artistic hopes lay with his biblical play, which was scheduled to open in June 1892. Sarah Bernhardt arrived in London and began rehearsals; although nearly fifty years old she intended performing the dance of the seven veils herself. The production was almost ready when it was announced that it had been banned. The English theatre was censored by the Lord Chamberlain's office, which was empowered to refuse a license to perform a play on a number of grounds. One of these, originally introduced in the Reformation to suppress Catholic mystery plays, forbade the use of Biblical characters. Whilst Bernhardt was annoyed with Wilde for not obtaining the licence earlier, his own anger ran much deeper. 'Salome' was the work that he fully expected would establish his reputation as a serious European man of letters rather than a writer of popular comedies. In his rage he turned on his adopted homeland, threatening to renounce his British citizenship and move to France.

'Since it is impossible to have a work of art performed in England, I shall transfer myself to another fatherland, of which I have long been enamoured,' he announced to a French journalist. 'Here people are essentially anti-artistic and narrow minded ... No doubt I have English friends to whom I am deeply attached; but as to the English I do not love them. There is a great deal of hypocrisy in England which you in France very justly find fault with.'

This was all hot air and bluff of course, since the English theatre provided Oscar's main source of income. Nonetheless he had just cause for complaint with the censor. The rule was an antiquated anachronism, which applied only to the theatre. It was perfectly legal to publish the text of 'Salome' in book form. Oscar was equally enraged that the Lord Chamberlain's office had allowed the staging of a sketch named 'The Poet and the Puppeteers'. In this satire, he complained, 'an artist dressed up like me and imitated my voice and manner.' The critic William Archer, one of Oscar's few supporters in the argument, took up the point. In a letter to the *Pall Mall Gazette* he stated: 'A serious work of art, accepted, studied and rehearsed by the greatest actress of our time, is peremptorily suppressed, at the very moment when the personality of its author is being held up to ridicule, night after night, on the public stage, with the full sanction of statutory infallibility.'

Oscar had little hope of overturning the censor's decision, and the dispute soon petered out. Yet the banning of the play did his reputation harm because there was a widespread belief that 'Salome' was banned because of its indecency. Curiously the only production of the play in Wilde's lifetime took place whilst he was languishing in Reading Gaol. In February 1896 'Salome' was staged in Paris, at a theatre managed by Oscar's friend Stuart Merrill. Whilst the actors' performances were barely adequate, the news that 'Salome' had at last been placed before the public encouraged its author while at his lowest ebb. Sarah Bernhardt, in contrast, behaved disgracefully to Oscar during his catastrophe. Before his 1895 trial Wilde sent Robert Sherard to ask the actress to buy the rights of the 'Salome' for £400, so that he could avoid being declared bankrupt. The actress refused, and fobbed off Sherard with empty promises to send money on later. 'Salome' continued to have a troubled history after Wilde's death. Although performed privately in England in 1906 to secure its copyright, the play did not receive its first public performance there until 1931, when it was staged at the Lyceum Theatre in London.

'Salome' remains the most elusive of Oscar's mature plays. It is a work of little movement, save in the famous dance before Herod, and its extravagant language can only be compared to some of Oscar's more ornate fairy tales. It has been suggested that the extraordinary style of the dialogue, which has a strangely repetitive, almost child-like quality, is partly a result of Oscar's limited command of French as a theatrical language. Wilde described his play as 'Byzantine', but a more astute description might be that of Sarah Bernhardt, who saw it as 'a fresco' rather than an orthodox drama. It is indeed a linked chain of posed scenes, culminating in set pieces like Salome's 'dance of the seven veils', her monologue to the head of the Baptist (Jokanaan), and finally her crushing to death beneath the shields of Herod's soldiers. The plot embroiders the bare bones of the New Testament story with a decadent sensuality. Salome's motive for wishing Jokanaan's death is her rejected passion for him. Herod also is impelled by sexual desire; he has no wish to execute the prisoner, and only does so after his lust for Salome allows her to trick him. Although the play was dismissed as drivel in England, it was perceived in Europe as a defining masterpiece of the *fin de siècle* period. It enjoyed huge success in France and Germany in the early 1900s, and largely accounts for its author's literary reputation in Europe, where he is more highly regarded as a writer than in England. Wilde's 'Salome' was the source for the libretto of the world-famous opera by Richard Strauss. This work, which used an abbreviated German translation of the play, was first staged in Berlin in 1905, with the renowned prima donna, Marie Wittrich, in the leading role.

'Salome' must be considered Wilde's most influential literary work outside England, but it also represented a blind alley in his career. His flirtation with the Symbolist movement ended in 1894, with the publication of 'The Sphinx', a long poem that he had been toying with since 1874. Henceforth, as Bosie's demands on his time and finances intensified, most of Oscar's creative energies would be poured into writing lucrative comedies for the English stage. And as he reached the pinnacle of his fame, his increasingly open liaison with Douglas pushed him ever closer to public exposure as a homosexual.

CHAPTER VIII

*I*MPENDING DISASTER

Oscar published a story in 1891 called 'Lord Arthur Savile's Crime', in which an English nobleman is told by a palm reader that he is going to commit a murder. The fiction had a strange counterpart in its author's life, when in April 1893 the renowned palmist Cheiro examined his hands after a dinner party. Cheiro told Wilde that whilst his left hand indicated tremendous success, his right hand suggested impending disaster. 'The left hand is that of a king, but the right hand that of a king who will send himself into exile.' With uncanny accuracy Cheiro predicted that this unspecified disaster would happen around his subject's fortieth year, which for Oscar would be 1895. The writer was unsettled by this disturbing information, and left the party without saying another word.

It was ironic that this incident happened on the night following the opening of 'A Woman of No Importance', the second of his extraordinarily successful comedies. The play was commissioned in the spring of 1892 by Oscar's old friend Herbert Beerbohm Tree, the greatest English stage personality of the era after Sir Henry Irving. Tree, the actor-manager of the Haymarket Theatre, hoped to emulate his rival George Alexander's triumph with 'Lady Windermere's

Fan'. Oscar wrote his new play in Germany (where he was recuperating from an illness) and at a rented farmhouse in Norfolk. Douglas was with him for most of this time, whilst Constance and the children stayed at Babbacombe Cliff with Lady Mount Temple. Wilde finished a 'Woman of No Importance' in the middle of October 1892, and handed the completed manuscript over to Tree in London.

After rehearsals in March 1893, which were punctuated by Oscar's efforts to interfere with Tree's direction, the play opened on 19 April 1893. 'A Woman of No Importance' proved even more popular than its predecessor. Oscar did not make a speech at the end of the first performance, but merely rose from his box to say to the audience: 'Ladies and Gentlemen, I regret to inform you that Mr Oscar Wilde is not in the house.' His new-found modesty pleased the critics he had offended on the opening night of 'Lady Windermere's Fan', and their reviews of the new play were somewhat more favourable. Wilde's reputation was further enhanced on the next evening, when the Prince of Wales came to see the play. The Prince, hearing of plans to shorten the play, told its author not to change a single line. Oscar reportedly replied 'Sire, your wish is my command,' and later voiced his pleasure at the Prince's tolerance: 'What a splendid country where princes understand poets.' Audiences, unfortunately, were less understanding than the future monarch. There had been some anger in the audience on the previous night at an unpatriotic line stating that 'England lies like a leper in purple'. Shortly afterwards it was taken out of the play.

The plot of 'A Woman of No Importance', as in 'Lady Windermere's Fan', revolves around a child who does not

117

know another character is a missing parent. This time there is an overt villain in Lord Illingworth, who wishes to take his grown-up son Gerald from Mrs Arbuthnot, 'a woman of no importance' whom he made pregnant and betrayed many years previously. Mrs Arbuthnot has told Gerald that his father is dead, and cannot reveal Illingworth's wicked treatment of her. She tries to persuade Gerald that his benefactor is an evil man, but he will not listen. Her dilemma is resolved when Lord Illingworth 'insults' Hester Worsley, an American friend of Arbuthnot's, presumably by sexually assaulting her. Gerald is about to attack the peer when his mother stops him, and reveals that Illingworth is his father. Lord Illingworth proposes marriage to Mrs Arbuthnot, hoping that this will keep his son close to him, but she refuses him with the support of Hester. The American girl becomes engaged to Gerald, who rejects his father in favour of his mother. The last act concludes with Mrs Arbuthnot slapping Illingworth with his glove, after which she dismisses him as 'a man of no importance'.

Oscar did not attach great importance to the plot of 'A Woman of No Importance', which is weak even by the standards of his other comedies.

'Plots are tedious,' he wrote to Herbert Beerbohm Tree about the play, 'anyone can invent them. Life is full of them. Indeed one has to elbow one's way through them as they crowd across one's path ... People love a wicked aristocratic who seduces a virtuous maiden, and they love a virtuous maiden for being seduced by a wicked aristocrat. I have given them what they like, so that they may learn to appreciate what I have given them.'

What distinguishes the play is the never-ending flow of its epigrams, witticisms and social comments. These include many of Oscar's most famous quotes, for instance: 'All women become like their mothers. That is their tragedy. No man does, that is his', 'Moderation is a fatal thing: nothing succeeds like excess', and 'The English country gentleman galloping after a fox – the unspeakable in pursuit of the un-eatable'.

Much of the play's bantering humour, in keeping with its underlying theme, is concerned with the battle of the sexes. Many of the best epigrams are given to Lord Illingworth, who shares Oscar's cynicism about women and marriage. 'Men marry because they are tired, women because they are curious. Both are disappointed,' he says, or 'The history of women is the worst tyranny the world has ever known. The tyranny of the weak over the strong. It is the only tyranny that lasts.' Perhaps the best exchange is between Illingworth and the character Mrs Allonby, on the terrace of Hunstanton Chase – the country house where the first three acts are set.

Lord Illingworth: Shall we go in to tea?
Mrs Allonby: Do you like such simple pleasures?
Lord Illingworth: I adore simple pleasures. They are the
    last refuge of the complex. But, if you wish, let us stay
    here. Yes, let us stay here. The Book of Life begins with
    a man and woman in a garden.
Mrs Allonby: It ends with Revelations.

The huge receipts from 'A Woman of No Importance' al-lowed Oscar to relax in luxury for most of 1893. He was be-ginning to spend long periods away from the house in Tite

Street, staying instead in luxurious London hotels like the Savoy and the Albermarle. His excuse to Constance was that he needed privacy to work, but in reality he was deserting her for Bosie and his rent boys. Whilst his relationship with Douglas was intense, their bonds were intellectual and emotional as well as sexual. Neither man was monogamous, and the lovers had other liaisons, both with rent boys and members of their own class. Wilde was involved with a number of young male prostitutes, including a boy named Charles Parker, whom he continued to see intermittently for several years. He brought another of his favourites, a youth named Sidney Mavor, on a holiday to Paris, where they openly stayed at the best hotels.

In 1893 Bosie foolishly left some love letters from Wilde in a coat he gave to Alfred Wood, a rent boy frequented by both men. One of Wood's friends attempted to sell one of the letters back, claiming that he could get £60 for it elsewhere. Wilde successfully laughed off the threat, but it was a potent warning. Wood returned all but the most incriminating letter shortly afterwards, and was given £30 to go to the United States. Yet the existence of that last letter from Wilde to Douglas – the 'Hyacinth letter' as it is usually known – posed an ongoing threat. Oscar attempted to reduce the danger of its being used against him. He arranged for his friend Pierre Louys to make a French translation, and published it in *The Spirit Lamp* (an Oxford magazine edited by Douglas) as 'a letter written in prose poetry by Mr Oscar Wilde to a Friend'. This may have temporarily deflected the blackmailers, but Wilde would later have to defend the Hyacinth letter in court.

Wilde's involvement with the petulant and often insolent

Bosie estranged him from several of his former associates. By the spring of 1893 the affair had brought about a split with his previous lover, John Gray, who formed a bond with the novelist André Raffalovich. Eventually Gray turned to religion and became a Catholic priest. The French writer, Pierre Louys, visiting Wilde and Douglas at the Savoy, was present when Constance called one morning with the post. He looked on in horror as she begged her husband to come home and see his children. Oscar joked that he had forgotten the number of his house since he had last been there, and she was reduced to tears. Afterwards he told the disgusted Frenchman that he had been married three times, once to a woman and twice to a man. In Paris, a few months later, Louys confronted Oscar over the incident. Wilde replied that he had no right to judge him, after which his former friend broke off all communications.

The affair was punctuated with quarrels caused by Bosie's erratic and self-centred personality. In June of 1893 he dropped out of Oxford after failing to appear for his Greats examination, and his demands became even more exorbitant. Oscar had rented a house at Goring-on-Thames earlier in the year, where he was beginning work on a new play. Bosie distracted his lover from writing with requests for attention, money and presents, and threw tantrums whenever he could not get his own way. Oscar finally reached the end of his tether after Douglas made a scene, and then stormed off vowing never to return. He returned three days later and was forgiven, but Wilde was losing patience with him. A worse quarrel followed in the autumn, when Oscar decided to translate 'Salome' into English, following the simultaneous publication of the French text in London and Paris. He asked Bosie, whose limited poetic talents he had consistently overestimated, to undertake this important project. The result was a disaster, since the younger man's command of the French language was inadequate. The translation was riddled with errors, and Wilde insisted on so many changes that Douglas was enraged. The two lovers stopped speaking, and Bosie refused to have anything more to do with 'Salome'. Aubrey Beardsley, the book's illustrator, further muddied the waters by offering his own translation, but this did not satisfy Oscar either. The breach between the lovers was only healed after Robbie Ross intervened at Bosie's request to settle their differences. Oscar eventually compromised over the botched translation by omitting Douglas's name from the title page of the published book, whilst acknowledging his contribution in a special dedication.

It was Robbie Ross's suggestion that Aubrey Beardsley, a precociously brilliant artist who was only twenty-one years old at the time, should illustrate the English translation. Oscar's dealings with the artist, who was undertaking his first major commission with 'Salome', were not easy. The sardonic Beardsley included four mocking caricatures of the author, portraying him as 'The Woman in the Moon' in one picture, and a court jester in another. Wilde, disliking the illustrations, dismissed them as 'the naughty scribbles a precocious schoolboy might make on the margins of his copybook'. He was equally scathing about their artist. 'They are cruel and evil, and so like dear Aubrey, who has a face like a silver hatchet, with grass-green hair,' he said. Nonetheless he restrained his annoyance and did not try to interfere with the artist's work. Beardsley's decorations and illustrations caused a sensation when the English translation of 'Salome' was published in 1894. Today they are considered master-pieces, and are far better known in England than the play for which they were commissioned.

Oscar's difficulties with Bosie were compounded by Queensberry's antagonism to the relationship. The Marquess was enraged at his son's leaving Magdalen, and blamed Wilde for distracting him from his studies. The Marquess was going through several other crises and could not turn his full attention on Lord Alfred, but it was a bad sign for the future. Queensberry's extreme homophobia was focused elsewhere for the moment. His eldest son, Francis, Viscount Drumlanrig, was private secretary to Lord Rosebery, the Foreign Minister in Gladstone's government. The Marquess, having convinced himself that there was an improper relationship between the two men, turned his attentions to harassing Rosebery. In August 1893 he went so far as to follow the Foreign Minister to Germany, where he attempted to assault him with a dog-whip. The Prince of Wales intervened, and had the Marquess deported back to England, but the accusations greatly distressed Drumlanrig. A few months later Queensberry was at the centre of another scandal, when he married a young woman named Ethel Weedon. His new wife ran away within days, and initiated divorce proceedings on the grounds that her new husband was impotent. Queensberry's anger at his latest humiliation was soon to be directed towards his estranged sons.

Oscar's discontent was brought to a head when Bosie and Robbie Ross were implicated in a serious sex scandal. It involved, Max Beerbohm wrote to his friend Reggie Turner, 'a schoolboy with wonderful eyes, Bosie, Bobbie (Ross), a furious father, George Lewis, a headmaster (who is now blackmailing Bobbie), St John Wontner, Calais, Dover, Oscar Browning, Oscar, Dover, Calais, and returned cigarette cases.' The father of Philip Danney, the sixteen-year-old boy at the centre of the affair, was only deterred from pressing charges by the discovery that his son would be imprisoned along with his seducers. The scandal temporarily drove Ross from England, and it was clear that Bosie should also make himself scarce for a while. Oscar used the opportunity to break with his tiresome lover and wrote a letter to Lady Queensberry. He suggested she send her son to Egypt:

'I think that, if he stays in London, he will not come to any good, and may spoil his young life irretrievably, quite ir-retrievably ... I like to think myself his greatest friend – he, at any rate makes me think so – so I write to you quite frankly to ask you to send him abroad to better surroundings.'

Lady Queensberry was as worried about her son as Oscar, and agreed to finance the trip. Bosie arranged his departure, but, being who he was, would not go easily or without tantrums. In fact he refused to leave at first without being reconciled Wilde, who stated that their intimacy was at an end. But eventually he was packed off to Cairo, and with a sigh of relief Oscar settled down to complete work on 'An Ideal Husband', which he had been unable to finish with Douglas hovering around his shoulders. Over the next three months he finished that comedy, and the one-act plays 'A Florentine Tragedy' and 'La Sainte Courtisane'. Wilde wanted nothing to do with Douglas now, and refused to answer the constant stream of letters from Cairo that arrived at his door. Bosie was by no means unhappy in Egypt, especially since he had been joined by several of his London friends, but he could not let the older man go. He wrote to his mother, and persuaded her to go to Tite Street and seek a reconciliation with Wilde on his behalf. Oscar would not be moved, and in desperation Bosie wrote to Constance. Constance was moved by the young man's heart-rending pleas and intervened with her husband, but Oscar still refused to write to him. After three months in Egypt, Douglas was offered a post at the British Embassy in Istanbul and took ship for Turkey. In Athens, however, he changed his mind and headed for Paris, from where he bombarded Oscar with requests to be allowed to return.

Wilde ignored him, but then Bosie played his trump card and sent a telegram threatening suicide. This was a serious matter given the history of the Douglas family, and Oscar went immediately to Paris, with the encouragement of Constance, for 'one last interview' with his rejected lover. He described what happened in 'De Profundis':

'When I arrived in Paris, your tears, breaking out again and again all through the evening, and falling over your cheeks like rain as we sat, at dinner first at Voisin's, at supper at Paillard's afterwards; the unfeigned joy you evinced at seeing me, holding my hand whenever you could, as though you were a gentle and penitent child; your contrition, so simple and sincere at the moment, made me consent to renew our friendship.'

It was a momentous decision in his life. Bosie was forgiven, and the two men returned to London together. The resumption of the affair was probably inevitable given the complementary natures of the two – which the poet W. H. Auden described as the Overloved meeting the Underloved. But the role of surrogate parent to Douglas would soon entangle Oscar in his companion's nightmarish love-hate relationship with Queensberry, and bring the full force of the father's wrath and malice against him.

Queensberry threw the figurative gauntlet down a few days after Douglas returned to London. On 1 April he entered the Café Royal to find Bosie and Oscar lunching together, in defiance of his strict orders to his son. Bosie persuaded his father to join them, and Oscar was able to calm down the aggrieved Marquess. By a supreme effort of charm he temporarily won over his lover's father – 'I don't wonder you are so fond of him, he is a wonderful man,' Queensberry told Douglas when he left the table – but on returning home he had second thoughts. The Marquess sat down and composed one of the bullying letters for which he was notorious.

'Secondly I come to the more painful part of this letter – your intimacy with this man Wilde,' he wrote. 'It must either stop, or I will disown you and cut off all money supplies. I am not going to try to analyse this intimacy, and I make no charge. But to my mind to pose as a thing is as bad as to be it. With my own eyes I saw you both in the most loathsome and disgusting relationship as expressed by your manner and expression …'

Further on in the letter he made the untrue allegation that Constance was about to divorce Wilde for sodomy, and threatened to shoot him on sight if this were true.

Bosie's reaction to this letter was to send back a telegram saying simply 'WHAT A FUNNY LITTLE MAN YOU ARE.' His childish response infuriated Oscar, who recognized that Queensberry was an extremely dangerous adversary. Queensberry composed a second letter to Bosie: 'If I catch you again with that man,' he wrote, 'I will make a public scandal in a way you little dream of; it is already a suppressed one. I prefer an open one.' In retrospect Oscar blamed Douglas for this disastrous exchange of messages, which he believed inflamed Queensberry to pursue his feud with him.

'When your father first began to attack me it was as your private friend ...,' he wrote in 'De Profundis'. 'You had already, before you saw me on the subject, sent your father a foolish and vulgar telegram ... That telegram conditioned the whole of your subsequent relations with your father, and consequently the whole of my life ... From pert telegrams to priggish lawyers' letters was a natural progress ... You left him no option but to go on ... If his interest had flagged for a moment your letters and postcards would soon have quickened its ancient flame. They did so.'

In the aftermath of this latest quarrel with his father Douglas fled to Florence for a month, where he was shortly afterwards joined by Oscar. On their return to London he employed the solicitor Charles Humphreys to represent him, since his old friend George Lewis was already representing Queensberry. Letters were exchanged, and the Marquess threatened to contact Scotland Yard if Oscar and Bosie did not break off their association. On 30 June 1894

Queensberry arrived at Oscar's house in Tite Street, accompanied by one of his prize-fighter friends. What followed in the ensuing confrontation is unclear. Wilde asserted that he faced the intruder down and threw him out of the house, with orders to his servant not to admit him again. 'I do not know what the Queensberry rules are, but the Oscar Wilde rule is shoot at sight,' he later claimed to have told his unwanted visitor. Queensberry, on the other hand, stated that Wilde had broken down, and promised to end his friendship with Bosie. In either event Oscar left London soon after, to spend the summer with Constance and the children in a small house in the seaside resort of Worthing, where he intended writing a new comedy that had been commissioned by George Alexander. The work went well over the summer months and he completed 'The Importance of Being Earnest', and sketched out another play that he would never complete. Bosie, to the relief of Constance, only came down to Worthing for one visit, and lodged in a nearby hotel rather than her small rented house. Whilst he was there Oscar picked up a local youth named Alphonso Conway, whom he afterwards took on a trip to Brighton.

Oscar's finances were once again in a perilous condition. He had staged no new plays since 1893, and could expect little profit from the English translation of 'Salome' and his long poem 'The Sphinx', the two books he published in 1894. His near poverty could be blamed on Bosie's extravagance. 'My ordinary expenses with you for an ordinary day in London – for luncheon, dinner, supper, amusements, hansoms and the rest of it – ranged from £12 to £20,' Oscar afterwards complained bitterly. 'For our three months at Goring my expenses (rent of course included) were £1,340 ... My expenses for eight days in Paris for myself, you, and your Italian servant were nearly £150: Paillard alone absorbing £85.'

As the summer of 1894 passed into autumn, the shadows began to gather around the playwright. Oscar was still in Worthing when he read that his old procurer, Alfred Taylor, was amongst eighteen men arrested in a raid on a private club in London. The hostile reaction of the public to this affair afforded further warning of the dangers he was courting in using rent boys. Then his publishers Lane and Mathews informed him they were unwilling to bring out his collected short stories because of the implied homosexual content of 'The Story of Mr W. H.'. A further indignity came in September, when Robert Hichens, a minor member of Wilde's circle, published his novel *The Green Carnation*, which satirized the two lovers under the pseudonyms of Esme Amarinth and Lord Reginald Hastings. In more normal circumstances this would have been merely amusing, and indeed some of Oscar's friends thought he had written the book himself as a joke. But it increased the already swelling gossip, and drove Queensberry to distraction. He was seen prowling the clubs and restaurants of London with his bruisers, on the look-out for Douglas and his lover.

As the external pressures on the relationship mounted, Douglas's sporadic cruelty to his lover led to their worst quarrel yet. In October 1894 he persuaded Oscar to bring him on holiday to the luxurious Hotel Metropole in Brighton. Soon after their arrival the younger man caught flu, and for almost a week Oscar tended to his every need. After his recovery Bosie moved to another lodging, so that Oscar could continue working on his new play. But then he too came down with the virus, and had to take to his bed. Bosie, in contrast to his own treatment, behaved vilely to the patient. He ignored Oscar, and when asked for a glass of water told him to get it for himself. Eventually he moved to another room in the hotel, abandoning the feverish and bed-ridden playwright. On 16 October, the day of his fortieth birthday, Oscar received a vicious letter from Bosie saying he had charged his hotel bill to Oscar's account. 'When you are not on your pedestal you are not interesting,' Bosie concluded, 'The next time you are ill I will go away at once.'

Oscar was deeply offended, and prepared to break off the relationship. He had given much to Douglas, in time, in energy, in money, and above all in his love. Bosie's obnoxious disloyalty in Brighton, and his subsequent insolence, was the last straw. He made ready to approach Queensberry's solicitor and tell him he agreed to end the friendship. Oscar was on the brink of finally ridding himself of Douglas when fate once more intervened. On the morning of 19 October, as he was about leave Brighton, Oscar read in his newspaper that Viscount Drumlanrig, Bosie's brother, had shot himself on the previous day. The viscount's suicide, for it was undoubtedly that, could largely be attributed to the rumours about his relationship with Rosebery circulated by his own father. Oscar felt unable to turn his back on Bosie in these tragic circumstances. 'My own griefs and bitterness against you I forgot,' he later wrote, '... I felt that to abandon you at that particular moment, and formally through a solicitor, would have been too terrible for you.'

As 1894 reached its end Oscar remained as close as ever to Douglas. He was already preparing for the opening of 'An Ideal Husband' at the Haymarket theatre in January 1895. At the rehearsals, which began in December, he drove the actors to distraction with his demands for perfection, even insisting that they work through Christmas Day. Wilde was also putting the finishing touches on 'The Importance of Being Earnest', which was due to open at the St James's Theatre in February. During the coming year Oscar should have experienced the greatest theatrical peak of his career. Instead he found himself dragged down into an abyss of suffering. Queensberry, maddened by the suicide of the estranged son who had not spoken to him for over a year, blamed his death on 'queers like Rosebery'. He was more committed than ever to ending the affair between Oscar and Bosie, no matter what the cost. Bosie was as determined to revenge himself on the father he now hated with all his being, and did not care who else might be destroyed in the process. Oscar, the helpless pebble trapped between the implacable millstones of Queensberry and Lord Alfred, was about to be ground into dust.

CHAPTER IX

*T*HE 'WILDE SCANDAL'

The year 1895 opened with a flourish for Wilde, when 'An Ideal Husband' opened at the Haymarket Theatre on 3 January in front of an audience that included the Prince of Wales and the Prime Minister of England, Alfred Balfour. The play was another stunning success, and the demand for tickets was so great that within a fortnight the management began running morning shows on Wednesdays and Saturdays. In all it ran for 111 performances before being taken off on the day after Wilde's arrest, and undoubtedly it would have played much longer but for that fact. The play began its New York run on 12 March 1895, where it was better received than any of Oscar's earlier plays.

'An Ideal Husband', which may be described as the last of Wilde's 'pink lampshade plays', has blackmail as its main theme. The villainous Mrs Cheverly threatens Sir Robert Chiltern, a Member of Parliament, with exposure for an earlier financial indiscretion if he does not withdraw a damaging report on the fraudulent Argentine Canal Company. He initially agrees, but is later persuaded to change his mind by his wife and writes a letter to Mrs Cheverly. Meanwhile Lord Goring, a suitor of Chiltern's sister Mabel, discovers a lost bracelet that belongs to the blackmailer. Mrs Cheverly deliberately lets Lady Chiltern overhear a conversation in which she reveals Chiltern's previous fraud, causing a rift between the couple. Then Lord Goring, who was once briefly engaged to Mrs Cheverly, intervenes to save Chiltern's political career. He snaps the lost bracelet around her wrist, and reveals that he knows she stole it from one of his relatives ten years previously; if she does not cease her blackmail he will have her arrested as a thief. Mrs Cheverly reluctantly agrees and returns Chiltern's letter, but as she leaves, announces she has stolen an incriminating note to Goring from Lady Chiltern, and will send it to her husband. The letter arrives in the last act of the play, but Chiltern assumes it is a conciliatory message to him from his wife. They are reconciled, but decide he should leave politics because of the earlier fraud. Goring persuades the Chilterns to change their minds, and the play concludes with Lord Chiltern accepting a seat in the cabinet, which he has been offered after his speech in Parliament denouncing the Argentine Canal Company.

Wilde's plot was probably inspired by Mark Twain and C. D. Warner's novel *The Gilded Age*, which features an adventuress called Laura Hawkes who blackmails an American senator. But Oscar's choice of blackmail as a subject also reflected his own unpleasant experiences with Alfred Woods and his cronies over the Hyacinth letter. Perhaps this dampened his usually buoyant spirits, since 'An Ideal Husband' is the most serious of his stage hits of the 1890s. There are fewer epigrams and witticisms, and it is perhaps the least enjoyable of the four.

There was a break of just over a month before 'The Importance of Being Earnest' opened in London. Wilde used the time to take Bosie on a short holiday to Algeria. Their choice of destination was due to French North Africa's reputation as a centre for what is now called 'sex tourism', the main attraction being the availability of Arab boys. The lovers spent a few days in the resort town of Blidah, and then returned to Algiers for the rest of Oscar's stay in the country. The French writer André Gide met the two men at this time, as he related in his autobiographical memoir *Si le grain ne meurt*. Gide spent several days in Oscar's company, after Douglas became infatuated with an Arab boy and deserted his companion. Wilde's conversation was as scintillating as ever, but the Frenchman was amazed at his openness about his relationship with Douglas. One night Wilde brought Gide to a café, where two teenage Arab musicians played for them. Afterwards Wilde arranged to meet the boys at a male brothel – roaring with laughter when his suspicions that Gide shared his sexual inclinations were confirmed. Douglas was absent when Oscar had to return to London, so Gide accompanied the playwright to his ship. He was in a fatalistic mood, unsure of what might be waiting for him in England as a result of his liaison with Bosie. 'I can't go any further,' he said to the French writer. 'Now something must happen.'

It would, but first Oscar would see the finest of his comedies produced. 'The Importance of Being Earnest' was a departure from his other plays, which had hung their humour on the bones of serious, if often shaky, dramatic plots. In the 'Importance of Being Earnest' Wilde cast off these restraints and indulged in pure farce. The result, as W. H. Auden described it, is 'verbal opera', a never-ending stream of witticisms and ludicrous misunderstandings. The plot concerns John Worthing, a foundling who has been brought up a country gentleman. In London, however, he pretends to be a fictitious younger brother, and calls himself Ernest Worthing. His ward Cecily Cardew declares herself in love with the non-existent Ernest (whom she knows only from Worthing's description), whilst his London fiancée Gwendolen Fairfax does not know that his real name is John. Then Gwendolen's cousin Algernon Moncrieffe discovers the secret, and pretends to be Ernest so he can woo Cecily. Following a comic series of misunderstandings John discovers he is really Ernest Moncrieffe, the infant brother of Algernon, Miss Prism, now Cecily's governess, accidentally having left him in a handbag at Victoria Station. The play ends with the couples happily united, and Gwendolen's domineering mother Lady Bracknell appeased.

'The Importance of Being Earnest' is the source of many celebrated quotations, including 'The truth is rarely pure and never simple', 'In married life three is company and two is none', 'Women only call each other sister when they have called each other lots of other things first', and 'To have lost one parent is a misfortune; to have lost both looks like carelessness'. Wilde's 'Trivial Comedy for Serious People' even delighted the London theatre critics, who were generally hostile to his plays. They considered it 'as new a new comedy as we have had this year' (*Pall Mall Gazette*), 'as bright and merry a piece of clever folly as was ever put on our stage' (*The Era*), and 'absurd, preposterous, extravagant, idiotic, saucy, brilliantly clever, and unedifyingly diverting' (*Daily Graphic*). With the spectacular launch of two plays within six weeks Wilde was confirmed as the uncrowned king of the English theatre.

Yet Queensberry's pursuit of Oscar was simultaneously

coming to its blundering crescendo. The irate Marquess turned up on the opening night of 'The Importance of Being Earnest' to disrupt the performance, but George Alexander had received word of his plans and prevented him from entering the theatre. 'He left a grotesque bouquet of vegetables for me!' Wilde wrote to Douglas in Algeria, 'This of course makes his conduct ridiculous, robs it of its dignity. He arrived with a prizefighter! I had all Scotland Yard – twenty police – to guard the theatre. He prowled around for three hours, and left chattering like a monstrous ape.' Bosie, as soon as he heard about the incident, abandoned his Arab boy and headed back to London. On the following day the Marquess provoked an even more serious incident. Oscar, having long since moved out of the house in Tite Street, was living at the Avondale Hotel in Piccadilly. Between four and five o'clock on the afternoon of 18 February, Queensberry called into the nearby Albermarle Club looking for his enemy. On finding Oscar was not there, he left a calling card with the hall-porter, on which he scribbled an insulting message. Queensberry was only semi-literate, and it is a curious sidelight on the fall of Oscar Wilde that the libel, the most famous in British legal history, is almost indecipherable. At his trial the Marquess claimed it read 'To Oscar Wilde – posing as a sodomite', but other possible interpretations of his message are 'posing sodomite' or 'ponce and sodomite'. Whatever the Marquess scrawled in his anger, he failed to spell sodomite correctly and wrote 'somdomite'.

Ten days passed, during which time Bosie returned from Algeria. Then Wilde walked into the Albermarle Club and was handed the offensive message. He now faced the greatest crisis of his life. The open insult appeared to leave Oscar with no choice but to retaliate. Yet he could probably have walked away without doing any further harm to his reputation. George Lewis later said that he would have advised Wilde to tear the card up and forget it. This was probably sound advice. It is unlikely that Queensberry left the message with any plan in mind – rather it was written in a rage after being foiled at the St James's Theatre on the previous evening. He may well have been happy to forget about the existence of the card, which had after all lain in the Albermarle Club for a week and a half without anybody mentioning it. For that matter Oscar could have dismissed the message as some unreadable scrawl from his pursuer.

But Wilde was not a man to be rational where his public name and social standing were concerned. Furthermore he knew that Queensberry would not stop harassing him until there was a public scandal. Oscar's initial reaction was to panic, and he returned to the Avondale Hotel intending to pack his bags and leave England. To his embarrassment he found that he could not afford to pay his bill, and was unable to check out. Oscar turned to his friend Robbie Ross. 'Since I saw you something has happened,' he wrote to him that afternoon, 'Bosie's father has left a card at my club with hideous words on it. I don't see anything now but a criminal prosecution. My whole life seems ruined by this man … ' Ross urged him to forget the matter, but Oscar went with Douglas to his solicitor W. H. Humphreys on the following morning. The meeting that followed opened a Pandora's box that could not be closed. Douglas was eager to take his father to court, and persuaded the more cautious Oscar to press charges. When Wilde pointed out that he had no money to pay for his legal costs, Bosie promised financial assistance from his mother and brother. At the end of the interview Humphries told his client that he could win a case against Queensberry, provided that there was no truth in the accusation. Wilde and Douglas denied they were homosexuals. It was a dangerous and reckless claim to make in the circumstances. 'What is loathsome to me is the memory of interminable visits paid by me to the solicitor Humphreys in your company,' he wrote bitterly afterwards, 'when in the ghastly glare of a bleak room you and I would sit with serious faces telling serious lies to a bald man, till I really groaned with ennui.'

Queensberry was arrested on 2 March 1895, and charged that 'he did unlawfully and maliciously publish a defamatory libel of and concerning one Oscar Wilde, at Albemarle Steet, on 18 February 1895.' The trial date was set for the Old Bailey on 3 April 1895, and Queensberry appointed the prominent barrister Sir Edward Carson to represent him. His private investigators commenced gathering evidence about Oscar's homosexual activities. One of their sources was the actor Charles Brookfield, author of the scurrilous sketch 'The Poet and the Puppeteer'. Brookfield, who was appearing in 'An Ideal Husband', passed on any gossip he knew about Oscar, against whom he harboured a bitter grudge. More names were received from a disgruntled female prostitute who resented the damage the rent boys were doing to her trade. The defence soon gathered evidence of thirteen separate homosexual encounters that would justify the allegation on Queensberry's card. The name of Lord Alfred Douglas, needless to say, was not on the list of young men identified as Oscar's sexual partners.

The impending libel trial jeopardized Oscar's position in Society even before it started. In an attempt to improve his standing he turned to Constance, and asked her to accompany him and Douglas to 'The Importance of Being Earnest' at the St James's Theatre. His abandoned wife was horrified by the scandal, but loyally agreed to participate in the charade. She also borrowed money from her relatives to help cover her husband's legal costs – knowing that he had just spent £1,000 on a trip to Monte Carlo with Douglas. Wilde was shown the information against him a few days before the trial was due to begin, giving him a chance to drop the charges. He refused to do so, despite the urging of Frank Harris and other sympathetic friends. Oscar's pride would not let him slip away so ignominiously. Instead he opted to risk being cross-examined; if he were to fall, let it be with a loud crash.

The Central Criminal Court of the Old Bailey was packed on the morning of 3 April when the trial of Queensberry began under the auspices of Mr Justice Collins. Queensberry – 'Standing there in a dark blue overcoat, short and dark, and mutton chop whiskered' – pleaded Not Guilty. Oscar's solicitor, Sir Edward Clarke Q.C., outlined the charges and then called the hall-porter of the Albermarle to confirm the time and place at which the offending card was received. The second witness was Oscar, who entered the courtroom wearing 'a dark chesterfield coat, and silk hat, and a dark tie'. He answered confidently as his barrister led him through the various events leading up to the libel. His evidence included an account of the attempted blackmail by Woods and his associates. Sir Edward read out the 'Hyacinth letter':

'My Own Boy, – Your sonnet is quite lovely and it is a marvel that those red-roseleaf lips of yours should be made no less for the madness of music and song than for the madness of kissing. Your slim built soul walks between passion and poetry ... Come here whenever you like. It is a lovely place and only lacks you ... Always with undying love – Yours OSCAR.'

Wilde denied that there was anything 'unclean' about the letter, and commented that he had told one of his attempted blackmailers; 'Ah, Art is rarely intelligible to the criminal classes.' The last part of his evidence was given over to defending *Dorian Gray* from the accusation of immorality, and ended with a denial of Queensberry's plea of justification. The *Star* succinctly summed up Oscar's bravura performance in its report of the first day's proceedings – 'The Aesthete Gives Characteristically Cynical Evidence, Replete with Pointed Epigram and Startling Paradox, and Explains His Views on Morality and Art.'

The defence cross-examination on the next day pitted Oscar against his former acquaintance Edward Carson. The barrister came from the same Anglo-Irish background as Oscar, and was the same age. He arrived in London in 1892 as the Member of Parliament for Trinity College, and two years later became the first Irish Q.C. to 'take silk' in England. Carson was an exceptionally brilliant man, perhaps one of the few in his generation whose intellect matched Wilde's. But he was a Unionist, and he had little sympathy for his fellow Irishman. He would do everything in his power to destroy Wilde on the witness stand.

Carson began by correcting Oscar on his real age, which he had stated on the previous day as 38. Having established he was in fact 40, Carson subtly pointed out the age difference between his witness and Douglas, and hinted at the unusual intimacy between the two men. He then moved on to question the witness about some overtly homosexual poems and prose pieces in an Oxford magazine called the *Chameleon*. Oscar got the best of these exchanges, by pointing out that he judged them only as literature. Carson asked 'I take it that you think ' "The Priest and the Acolyte" ' was not immoral?' 'It is worse, it is badly written,' Oscar replied. He scored again when Carson suggested *Dorian Gray* proved his unnatural attraction to young men. 'The passage I am quoting says ' "I quite admit that I adore you madly" '. Have you had that feeling?' Carson asked. Oscar's answer reduced the gallery to laughter: 'I have never given admiration to anybody but myself. The expression was, I regret to say, borrowed from Shakespeare.'

Carson now began to take the cross-examination on to more dangerous ground. He brought up the letters found by Wood, and read one of them out. Wilde again foiled him. To the question 'Is that an extraordinary letter?' he replied: 'I think that everything I write is extraordinary. I don't pose as being ordinary, great heavens! Ask me anything you like about it.' Slowly Carson turned his attention to Wilde's relationship to Woods and the other blackmailers. He established that Oscar was on first-name terms with Alfred Taylor, and then began introducing the names of some of the rent boys Oscar had been intimate with. Wilde hit back now and again, as when Carson sarcastically asked if it was an intellectual treat to dine with a youth named Edward Shelly – 'Yes, for him,' he replied. The negative impression caused by Oscar's interest in these men was reinforced when he admitted giving gifts to Alphonso Conway, the youth he met in Worthing.

The next day's cross-examination was even more devastating for Oscar. Carson delved more deeply into his links with Alfred Taylor, and introduced the names of more young working-class men Oscar had wined, dined and given money to. Wilde grew rattled, and finally made the mistake for which the barrister was hoping. Carson asked him if he had kissed one Walter Grainger, a servant of Bosie's. 'Oh dear no,' Oscar replied. 'He was a particularly plain boy. He was, unfortunately, extremely ugly. I pitied him for it.' 'Was that the reason why you did not kiss him?' Carson shot back, and Oscar's temper snapped. 'Oh, Mr Carson, you are impertinent and insolent.' It was too late for him to pretend moral indignation, for Carson had torn him to shreds on the witness stand. After some more questions about his relationships with other young men Carson dismissed him.

The destruction of Oscar's reputation on the second day of the trial was summed up by an article in the *Evening Standard*; '… even the Old Bailey recoiled with loathing from the long ordeal of terrible suggestion that occupied the whole of yesterday, when the cross examination left the artistic literary plane and entered the dim-lit, perfumed rooms where the poet of the beautiful joined with valets and grooms in the bond of the silver cigarette case.' On the next morning Carson began the defence of Queensberry. When he stated he was about to call on the men he had named on the previous day, Sir Edward Clark asked the judge's permission to confer with his opponent. Earlier in the morning, seeing that the case was lost, he had offered to keep the trial going so that Oscar could escape to France. But his client intended staying in England to answer the charges made by Carson, and the barrister had decided to concede the case.

Clarke hoped to soften the blow by persuading the defence to accept a Not Guilty verdict for the 'posing' part of the charge only. But Carson refused point-blank, and the jury was instructed to acquit Queensberry on the grounds that he had been justified in calling Oscar a sodomite. The Marquess left the courtroom to applause; it was perhaps the first time in his life that a London crowd had been on his side. Within minutes of his departure his solicitor was sending off the incriminating evidence he had gathered to the Director of Public Prosecutions.

Oscar was with Bosie, Ross and Reginald Turner at the Cadogan Hotel. At one point he was about to flee, then he changed his mind again. He would stay, whatever the cost, face his trial, and serve out any sentence that might follow his conviction. At 6.30p.m., about seven hours after the collapse of his case against Queensberry, two plain-clothes police officers came and took him into custody. Oscar, as immaculately polite with his social inferiors as ever, offered to pay the hansom cab fare to Scotland Yard, but the detectives informed him they were provided with money for that purpose. The cabby whipped up his horse, and the career of the most successful playwright in England came to an abrupt and permanent end.

Oscar was kept in custody through the initial hearings of his case, much to the detriment of his health, 'The fortnight's confinement in Holloway Gaol has told severely on Wilde,' the *Illustrated Police News* wrote of the committal hearing on 18 April. 'He has lost a great deal of flesh. His face looked almost bloodless, and his eyes heavy and weary.' Behind the scenes there was much legal activity, as the Director of Prosecutions prepared the case against the playwright. It was decided that he should stand trial with Alfred Taylor, the procurer of some of the rent boys involved in the case. None of these would stand trial for their admitted offences, since they were being offered immunity from prosecution and paid for their testimony. Another deal was made with Queensberry, who agreed to give evidence if Bosie was kept out of the trial. Charles Gill, the barrister for the Crown, justified the decision in a letter to the Director of Public Prosecutions.

'Having regard to the fact that Douglas was an undergraduate at Oxford when Wilde made his acquaintance – the difference in their ages – and the strong influence that Wilde has obviously exercised over Douglas since that time, I think that Douglas, if guilty, may fairly be regarded as one of Wilde's victims.'

Bosie had written to the papers defending Wilde, and even offered to testify in court that he had committed the sodomy offences that Wilde was falsely accused of (Oscar did not indulge in anal intercourse, but restricted himself to fondling and oral sex). But as always his behaviour was distorted by his hatred for his father, and Wilde's lawyers decided that his testimony would hinder the defence rather than help it. The malevolent Queensberry was still wreaking vengeance on Wilde. 'In my time I have cut up sharks ... ' he responded to suggestions that he had expressed sympathy for his enemy. 'I would treat him with all possible consideration as a sexual pervert of an utterly diseased mind, and not as a sane criminal.' Queensberry was instrumental in procuring Oscar's bankruptcy, when the money promised by Bosie's mother and brother failed to materialize. Wilde's creditors moved in quickly, and on 24 April an auction of his letters, papers, books and household effects was held in Tite Street. The lots ranged from a bundle of his typewritten manuscripts (sold for £5,15s), to sketches by Whistler, and such oddities as Thomas Carlyle's writing desk; Oscar's collection of 'old blue china and Moorish pottery', it was reported 'did not excite connoisseurs to high bidding'. The auction, which could have been avoided if Bosie's mother and his brother Percy had not reneged on their undertakings, stripped Wilde of most of his possessions. Moreover the proceeds did not come close to covering his debts, leaving him to face bankruptcy proceedings later in the year. 'The Law has taken from me not merely all I have ... everything in fact from ' 'The Happy Prince'' and ' 'Lady Windermere's Fan'' down to the stair carpet and door knocker of my house, but also all that I am ever going to have,' he later wrote. Wilde afterwards blamed his bankruptcy on Douglas, who suggested it as a means to thwart Queensberry, without caring about any of the later consequences.

The trial of Oscar and his co-accused, Taylor, on charges of gross indecency began on 26 April 1895, with Sir Edward Clarke leading the defence. The prosecuting counsel, Charles Gill, another graduate of Trinity College, Dublin, had no more liking for his countryman than his predecessor Carson. When Wilde was brought in he looked 'haggard and worn, and his long hair, which is usually so well kept, was dishevelled and untidy.' The prosecution case was based on the testimony of a succession of rent boys, who took the stand one by one to swear they had been intimate with the accused. They were an unsavoury lot for the most part, although one man, Sydney Mavor, stated he not been associated with Oscar. Several of the witnesses were revealed as blackmailers, whilst one male prostitute, Charles Atkins, was exposed as a perjurer when it was revealed he had been arrested for beating up and robbing a client. Oscar gave a superb performance on the witness stand. He defended his friendship with Bosie, who had been named as having introduced some of the rent boys to him. When asked about Douglas's poem 'Two Loves', Oscar made an eloquent speech praising 'a great affection of an elder for a younger man such as there was between David and Jonathan, such as Plato made the very basis of his philosophy, and such as you find in the sonnets of Michael Angelo and Shakespeare ... It is beautiful, it is fine, it is the noblest form of affection ... That it should be so the world does not understand. It mocks at it and sometimes puts one in the pillory for it.'

It seemed to neutral observers that both men would be convicted, but at the end of the trial one or possibly two of the jury held out against the majority, and it failed to reach a verdict. In other circumstances the accused might have been discharged, but public opinion was running high. 'In England,' as a bemused French commentator noted, 'pederasty is the worst crime after murder.' The newspapers scented a widespread homosexual conspiracy. 'Whatever may be the truth about Wilde and Taylor,' the editor of *The Morning* declared, 'the evidence given at the Old Bailey seems to affect more reputations than those that have been openly impugned. What are those mysterious names written on slips of paper and passed between counsel's table, the witness box and the Bench? If there is a widespread canker in our midst, as the authorities seem to believe, it cannot too soon be thoroughly cauterized.'

Comments like these left the authorities no choice but to re-try Oscar and Taylor. Not to do so would give credence to the whispered allegations about the sexual tastes of Lord Rosebery and his circle. Oscar was returned to Bow Street prison. A few days later he was allowed bail, and released to await his next trial. Oscar went to find a hotel, but Queensberry's hired thugs were following him, and intimidated the managers into turning him away. After being refused by several hotels he fled to the home of Lady Wilde, his last refuge in London. The old lady, by now well into her seventies, was living with her elder son Willie and his second wife. Oscar had not spoken to his brother following a quarrel nearly two years previously, but he was allowed entry. Nevertheless Willie was not kind to Oscar, and was heard to mutter 'at least my vices are decent'. He refused to eat with his brother, and instead dined out at his expense.

The next few weeks served as an interlude as Wilde waited for the next trial, and prepared himself for the prison sentence he expected to follow. W. B. Yeats, arriving from Dublin with messages of support from some of his fellow Irish writers, found Wilde determined not to flee. His mother was encouraging him to stay, whatever the cost: 'If you stay, even if you go to prison, you will always be my son. It will make no difference to my affection. But if you go, I will never speak to you again.' Friends like Frank Harris, on the other hand, advised him to escape, and prepared a yacht to carry him to safety in Europe. Constance spent two hours begging her husband to leave before the trial, and left in tears when he refused. On 20 May, the evening of his re-trial, Oscar said goodbye to the handful of loyal friends who had supported him through his ordeal, and gave each a small present from his few remaining possessions. He went to bed at peace with himself, prepared for whatever he might face on the morrow.

The second trial of Oscar Wilde was prejudiced from its outset by the hostility of the presiding judge, Mr Justice Willis. He began by deciding that Taylor should be tried first, which would leave the jury prejudiced against Oscar when it came to his turn. Taylor was rapidly found guilty, and then Oscar's case was heard. The evidence was broadly similar to the first trial, with the Parker brothers, Woods and the other rent boys the main prosecution witnesses. Edward Clarke, who was defending Oscar without a fee, managed to get the evidence of Edward Shelley, the only prosecution witness who was not a male prostitute, declared inadmissible. Yet in the general tide of hysteria there was little he could do to save his client. Halfway through the trial, Queensberry, who was still as much at odds with his sons as with Wilde, accosted his own son Percy in Piccadilly. The two ended up in a public brawl, were arrested, and bound over to keep the peace. Oscar was no doubt pleased to hear that his persecutor had got the worst of the exchange, and was sporting a black eye.

The trial ended on 25 May, after a stinging attack on Wilde by Sir Frank Lockwood, the Crown Solicitor. The jury retired at 3.30 in the afternoon, and returned two hours later to convict the accused man on all charges except those involving Edward Shelley. Wilde and Taylor were then brought to face the judge. Mr Justice Willis berated the prisoners, before sentencing them to two years' hard labour – the maximum penalty he was allowed to impose. 'Wilde appeared to be totally unable to realize what had happened'.

one reporter wrote of the playwright's reaction 'He leaned upon the rails of the dock and made a feeble attempt to say something, but checked himself on the touch of the warder by his side.' There was silence in the courtroom at the immensity of the tragedy they were now witnessing. 'The scene will for ever be a memorable one, and will remain in my mind as a vivid picture of a talented man, a learned scholar, and a great dramatist going to his doom – a doom to him more horrible than the gallows to a murderer', another observer wrote. Outside the court, as Yeats related in his autobiography, 'the whores danced on the pavement'. The activities of rent boys had damaged their business, and they were delighted at the severity of the sentences. The two prisoners were taken from the Central Criminal Court to the adjoining Newgate prison, where they waited until the van arrived to transport them to Holloway Prison. Within five short months Oscar Wilde had been transformed from the darling of London high society to England's most loathed and despised criminal.

The severity of the sentence was extraordinary, even by the standards of Victorian justice. The young men who testified against Oscar were his willing accomplices after all, and if they had been female prostitutes he would have faced little more than a fine. The motive behind the 'rough justice' meted out to him lay solely in the obsessive homophobia of the Victorian public. This sprang from the belief that homosexuality was widespread in the upper classes, for which schools like Bosie's old 'alma mater' Winchester College were blamed. An editorial in the *Star*, on the day after the case concluded, typified this attitude: 'Our second comment is that the lesson of the trial ought not to be lost upon the headmasters, and all others who are responsible for the morals of public schools. It rests with them, more probably than with anybody else, to exorcize this pestilence.'

The responsibility bringing the weight of the Law against Oscar lay with Queensberry and Bosie. The father's accusation that Oscar was a 'sodomite' led to the libel case, and culminated in his devastating exposure on the witness stand. The son's baiting provoked the feud, and by persuading his lover to take legal action in the first place he doomed him. Yet Wilde also brought catastrophe on himself by his arrogance and lack of discretion. Although he knew the infatuation with Douglas was dangerous, Oscar would not end it, even when he became a pawn in his lover's quarrel with the malevolent Queensberry. And his decision to remain in England and face trial, no matter how noble it might have seemed, was misguided. It is unlikely that Oscar would have courted martyrdom quite so easily if he had been aware of its price. The 'Wilde scandal' sent a terrifying warning to homosexuals in England, hundreds of whom fled to the Continent in its aftermath. England's shabby anti-homosexuality laws would not be repealed for over seventy years, during which time thousands of men would endure the same treatment from the police and courts as Oscar.

CHAPTER
X

ℐMPRISONMENT

Oscar Wilde's incarceration for two years in the English prison system was an ordeal from which he never recovered. When the convicted prisoner reached Holloway the guards took away his clothes and personal items. He was issued with the standard drab prison suit, with its broad arrows and shapeless 'Scottish cap'. On the following Monday he was removed to Pentonville Prison, where his hair was shaved off and he was subjected to a full medical examination. The doctor passed Oscar as healthy, and he was ordered to take his daily six hours shift on the treadmill. The hard labour exhausted the middle-aged prisoner, who was unused to any physical work. After a few days he fell sick with diarrhoea as a result of the bad food and dank cell in which he was placed. Oscar was then observed to be suffering from 'mental prostration and melancholy'. At first his psychological problems were ascribed to 'prison head', a state of mind caused in new prisoners by the effect of the medicine – containing potassium and bromide – forced upon them by the doctors. Oscar was excused from his dose, but his mental condition continued to decline. He was taken from his cell to the infirmary, and placed under twenty-four hour surveillance because the prison authorities feared he might be suicidal. Wilde was discharged following his partial recovery, and allotted 'second-class work', which consisted of picking oakum for ten hours a day in his cell. He was confined to his cell for twenty-three hours a day, and released only for one hour's exercise in the yard: during this period he was not allowed to converse with the other inmates. There were hardly any books in the prison library, and Oscar was not allowed to have paper and pen in his cell.

The harsh realities of prison life crushed Wilde's body and mind. The intention of a Victorian prison was to punish rather than rehabilitate, and the daily regime was harsh. Even for the habitual criminals who made up the bulk of the population of Pentonville it was almost unbearable. For Oscar, who was used to the highest circles of society, and had been well fed, well housed and pampered by servants all his life, the prison must have felt like the lowest circle of Hell. Mired in loneliness and misery, he was left with too much time to brood on his public disgrace, and became a ghost of his former extrovert self. Wilde turned into a broken-hearted melancholic, filled with self-pity and given to bouts of weeping. Towards the end of June he received his first visitor, R. B. Haldane, a member of the committee investigating prisons for the Home Office. Haldane, seeing Oscar's evident distress, offered him some comfort and promised to allow him a small number of suitable books. He also arranged for the prisoner to be transferred from Pentonville to Wandsworth, where conditions were thought to be marginally better.

Shortly afterwards Oscar received a visit from his brother-in-law Otho Holland. Constance and his children were now living in Switzerland, having been driven out of England by his disgrace. Otho indicated that Constance was considering a divorce, but might take him back after his sentence if he renounced his former vices. Oscar pinned his hopes on reconciling himself with his spouse, and asked Robert Sherard to contact her on his behalf. Constance cancelled the divorce proceedings and sent him an encouraging letter. On 21 September 1895 she returned from Switzerland to visit Oscar at Wandsworth Prison. It was a painful meeting for both of them, but ended with her agreeing to accept Oscar back when he was released from prison, provided he had nothing more to do with Douglas. 'He has been mad the last three years,' Constance wrote on the following day, 'and he says if he saw Lord A. he would kill him. So he had better keep away, and be satisfied with having marred a fine life. Few people can boast of so much.'

Wilde's opinion of Bosie soon changed in the wake of his conviction. In the months leading up to his imprisonment he had felt himself more intensely close to his paramour than ever before. When Douglas fled to France shortly before the final trial, Oscar sent a long farewell letter declaring his continuing affection. 'Dearest boy, sweetest of all young men,' he wrote at the end, 'most loved and most lovable. Oh! Wait for me! Wait for me! I am now, as ever since the day we met, yours devoutly and with an immortal love, Oscar.' After a few weeks enduring the horrors of prison, however, Wilde's mood hardened. He began to realize the harm that Bosie had done him, and the injustice of their respective situations. Douglas was enjoying his usual profligate lifestyle with some friends in Le Havre, with little more to worry about than the local mayor, who was complaining about his corruption of boys in the town. Having left Oscar to face trial and imprisonment alone, he was now proposing to publish an article about the affair in the review *Mercure de France*. He wrote to Wandsworth asked permission to quote from the intimate letters he had received from Wilde. The prisoner was furious at Douglas for his 'hideous rashness' in wanting to publish the article, which would wreck his delicate negotiations with Constance. Oscar refused permission to use his letters and the article was withdrawn.

On 22 September 1895, Wilde was taken from prison to witness the bankruptcy proceedings against him. He had amassed debts of over £3,500, almost a quarter of which were owed for Queensberry's legal costs. Notwithstanding the frantic efforts of Ross, Sherard and his other friends, no benefactor could be found to meet them. The true worthlessness of Bosie's friendship was revealed to Oscar at the Bankruptcy Court. Whilst he was waiting to be called before the judge, a solicitor's clerk sidled up to him. 'Prince Fleur de Lys wishes to be remembered to you,' he whispered, and seeing Oscar's confusion added, 'The gentleman is abroad at present'. Wilde remembered that 'Fleur de Lys' was a nickname he had given Bosie in the early days of their romance, and laughed derisively. His expenditure on satisfying Bosie's extravagant tastes over the previous three years exceeded £5,000. Bosie then encouraged him to sue Queensberry by promising help from his mother, Lady Queensberry. This financial help never materialized because Douglas advised her not to give Oscar anything – for the reason that the money would eventually go to his hated father. Bosie's only response to the desperate financial and legal situation he had manoeuvred his lover into was to bribe a court servant with a few sovereigns to deliver an inane message from the safety of France. As he left the courthouse after being declared a bankrupt, Oscar received a lesson in the nature of real friendship. Robbie Ross stepped out of the crowd waiting to jeer the infamous convict and raised his hat in greeting. His courageous public gesture in the hostile atmosphere touched the outcast, and contrasted starkly with Bosie's cowardly long-distance efforts at solace.

Wilde made it clear to Sherard and Ross that he wanted nothing more to do with Douglas. His mind was made up, and all he wished for was to resume his married life after prison. Oscar could never have been happy with Constance, but it was a straw to cling to as he was swept through the prison system. Bosie's response to his rejection was typically self-absorbed. 'I am not in prison,' he wrote, 'but I think I suffer as much as Oscar and in fact more, just as I am sure that he would have suffered more if he had been free and I in prison ... Doesn't he think my life is just as much ruined as his and much sooner?' In the following year Douglas tried to dedicate 'The City of the Soul', his first volume of poetry, to the prisoner. Wilde responded by sending a blistering message via Robbie Ross to demand that he do no such thing. He also asked for the return of all his letters and presents. 'I cannot of course get rid of the revolting memories of the two years I was unlucky enough to have him with me,' Oscar wrote to Ross, 'or of the mode by which he thrust me into the abyss of ruin and disgrace to satisfy his hatred of his father and other ignoble passions. But I will not have him in possession of my letters or gifts ... I will have nothing to do with him nor allow him to come near me.' Oscar's resentment at Bosie's betrayal of him would burst forth in a torrent of blame when he came to write 'De Profundis'.

155

In November 1895 it was decided to move Oscar to yet another prison. He was every bit as miserable at Wandsworth as at Holloway, and his mental and physical health were still in decline. Wilde had been deeply humiliated when the deputy chaplain made unfounded accusations that he had been masturbating in his cell. Although this man was relieved from duty by the prison authorities, some of the warders continued to treat Oscar badly. During one bout of sickness he was forced to go to chapel under threat of the severest punishment. He fainted during the service and fell, badly damaging his ear. Oscar spent two months in the prison infirmary, and the recurring ear infection he suffered from the accident contributed to his death some years later. After this latest misfortune Haldane again intervened, and Wilde was transferred to Reading Gaol. During his journey from Wandsworth he experienced the total nadir of his fortunes, as he described in 'De Profundis'.

'On November 13th 1895, I was brought down here from London. From two o'clock until half past two on that day I had to stand on the centre platform of Clapham Junction in convict dress, and handcuffed, for the world to look at. I had been taken out of the hospital ward without a moment's notice being given to me. Of all possible objects I was the most grotesque. When people saw me they laughed. Each train as it came up swelled the audience. Nothing could exceed their amusement. That was, of course, until they knew who I was. As soon as they had been informed they laughed still more. For half an hour I stood there in the grey November rain surrounded by a jeering mob. For a year after that was done to me I wept every day at the same hour and for the same space of time.'

At first Oscar found the new prison as uncomfortable as the last. The bed in his cell, number C. 3.3, was every bit as hard as those in Wandsworth, and the convicts' diet just as poor. Dysentery had weakened Wilde to the extent that he was judged unfit for hard labour. The authorities detailed him for less strenuous work in the garden and the prison library. At least Oscar was allowed to read in his cell, and permitted to order more books for himself. But Colonel Isaacson, the governor of Reading Gaol was a martinet, whom Wilde described as having 'the eyes of a ferret, the body of an ape and the soul of a rat'. Oscar soon fell foul of the innumerable petty regulations that Isaacson enforced against convicts. One day he was in the exercise yard when another prisoner whispered: 'Oscar Wilde, I pity you because you must be suffering more than we are.' He replied 'No, my friend, we are all suffering equally.' When the governor heard about the exchange he called Oscar and the other convict into his office. According to prison rules the one who spoke first was to receive a much harder punishment than the other, but Oscar took responsibility along with his fellow prisoner. Isaacson imposed severe penalties on both men.

In February of 1896 Wilde received tragic news, preceded by two omens. One afternoon a warder was sweeping out his cell for him when a spider scuttled out. He yelled out that killing it brought bad luck, but he was too late to prevent the beast being crushed underfoot. A couple of nights later he heard the cry of the banshee, the supernatural Irish spirit that warns of the death of a close relative. Almost a fortnight later Constance unexpectedly called at the prison. She was in ill health due to a spinal injury she had received after falling down the stairs at Tite Street several years before.

Nonetheless she had travelled all the way from Genoa to tell him personally that his mother was dead. Lady Wilde had been deeply upset by Oscar's imprisonment; in fact it had broken the old lady's heart, and she had barely gone out of doors for months. Wilde took much of the responsibility for her death on himself, although she had been weakening for several years before his disgrace. Constance comforted her grieving husband, but was shocked at his physical and mental condition: 'They say he is quite well, but he is an absolute wreck compared to what he was.'

In the aftermath of Lady Wilde's death Oscar fell into an even deeper depression, and began fearing for his sanity. In July 1896 he sent a letter to the Home Secretary, begging for his release on the grounds that he was on the verge of a complete mental breakdown: 'It is but natural that living in this silence, this solitude, this isolation from all human and humane influences, this tomb for those that are not yet dead, the petitioner should, day and night in every waking hour, be tortured by the fear of absolute and entire insanity.' The letter fell on deaf ears, and it is unlikely that Oscar could have survived much longer if things had continued as they were. Fortunately for Oscar the government of W. E. Gladstone was committed to the reform of Britain's nightmarish prisons, and took action to improve his situation. A new governor, Major J. O. Nelson, was appointed, and he made provisions to give the prisoner in C.3.3 a decent supply of books and the pen, paper and ink that might revive his dying spirit.

Wilde later called Nelson 'the most Christlike man I ever met', and it is almost certain that the new governor saved the sanity, and possibly the life, of his famous prisoner. He treated Oscar with decency and revived his faith in human nature. Nothing could stop the conditions in Reading Gaol being appalling, but the governor introduced a new spirit of humanity into its dark corridors, cells and workshops. Nelson's greatest contribution to Oscar's wellbeing was to offer him the opportunity to write again. The regulations only allowed a prisoner the use of writing materials for composing a letter, but the governor found a way of getting round this obstacle. Since no limit was placed on the length of the letter, he allowed Oscar to write one as long as he wished, provided that he surrendered each day's work as it was completed. From this came Wilde's most personal work – the long letter to Lord Alfred Douglas now known as 'De Profundis'.

Oscar's letter was written over a period of three months, from January to March 1897. Considering that he was not allowed to keep the pages as he wrote them it was a remarkable achievement for a man who was so mentally and physically exhausted. Cynics, reading the edited 1905 version released by Robert Ross, have described the document as 'Oscar Wilde's greatest piece of fiction', but this is due to a misunderstanding of his intention in writing it. 'De Profundis', in the form published in 1905, is a spiritual meditation, a renunciation of the carnal side of Oscar's nature for the consolation of religion. Ross's motives for not publishing the full letter were twofold; he wished to restore Oscar's reputation and he feared being sued by Douglas. But by deleting large sections of the text he left readers with a false impression of its content. Only with its full publication in 1962 could the letter be allotted a proper place in the canon of Oscar Wilde's literary works.

'De Profundis' is primarily Wilde's complaint against Douglas for bringing about his downfall. Oscar lays out the wrongs that Douglas has done him in the most exhaustive detail, dedicating eight printed pages of the full version of the letter to the quarrel in Brighton alone. He blames Bosie for sacrificing him in pursuit of his quarrel with Queensberry: 'In you Hate was always stronger than love. Your hatred of your father was of such stature that it entirely outstripped, o'erthrew and out shadowed your love of me.' The key to Oscar's mental anguish caused by his oscillating feelings about Bosie is clear in another passage. After attacking him viciously he writes: 'There is I know, one answer to all I have said to you, and that is that you loved me: that all through those two and a half years during which the Fates were weaving into one scarlet pattern the threads of our divided lives you really loved me. Yes I know you did. No matter what your conduct to me was I always felt that at heart you really did love me.'

From Oscar, the martyred lover, it was a short step to assuming the mask of Oscar, the crucified victim. As the letter progresses and he begins writing of his spiritual rebirth, Wilde's identification with Christ becomes more and more apparent. Some of the images from the section of 'De Profundis' where he writes of the Crucifixion, suggest how absolutely Oscar had created a Christ in his own image: '... he (Christ) ranks with the poets ... his entire life is also the most wonderful of poems', '... the false friend coming close to him so as to betray him with a kiss; the friend who still believed in him ... denying him as the bird cried to the dawn; his own utter loneliness, his submission, his acceptance of everything ...', 'the crucifixion of the innocent one before the eyes of his mother and the disciple whom he loved'. Yet his lyrical exposition on the nature of 'Christ as the precursor of the romantic movement in life' is sandwiched between his almost neurotic tirade against Bosie and his parents. 'De Profundis' is as much the cry of a wronged lover as an account of a religious awakening through suffering.

By the end of March, as he finished his long letter, the end of Oscar's two-year sentence was approaching. During these last few months Wilde's confinement was made easier by the kindness of his warder Thomas Martin, who left an account of the famous prisoner. Oscar had now become something of a celebrity in the prison. On one day a fellow prisoner came up in the exercise yard to whisper that he had been at all his first nights and trials (as if both were equally entertaining), whilst another embarrassed him by indicating he was a fellow Freemason in need of help. Oscar was now eagerly awaiting his release. He had several literary works in mind, including a play called 'Constance' about the loyalty of a betrayed wife. He knew he could not stay in England, and intended to make his home on the Continent. His wife had promised to provide him with a small allowance, and he hoped that in time she would allow him to rejoin her and his children. As his release date approached, Oscar became curiously irascible with Ross and his other friends, unjustly finding fault with the way they had looked after his financial and personal affairs during his prison sentence. He was being unreasonable, for it was not their fault if he would have to survive off of the generosity of his wife. Oscar had always been careless with money, and with the help of Bosie and the court case against Queensberry he had orchestrated his own financial downfall. Nothing could reverse that fact, and his bankruptcy would prevent him from reaping any future rewards from his efforts.

Oscar's experiences during his imprisonment convinced him that reforms were needed to redress the lack of compassion in the prison system. The mindless brutality shown to individual prisoners was underlined during his last days at Reading Gaol, when A.2.11, a mentally ill convict, was brutally whipped for 'malingering'. Oscar was even more shocked by the plight of three small children, who were imprisoned because nobody would pay their small fine for stealing some rabbits. He tried to find out their names from Warder Martin, so he could help them on his release. Afterwards Oscar found out that Martin, who was just as sorry for them, had given the youngest boy a biscuit. When his superiors found out the warder was immediately dismissed from the prison service. Oscar's concern with the welfare of his fellow inmates was reflected in a letter he wrote from France shortly after his release.

'My dear friend – I send you a line to show I haven't forgotten you … Don't, like a good little chap, get into trouble again. You would get a terrible sentence. I send you two pounds just for luck … There is also ten shillings which I wish you would give to the little dark-eyed chap who had a month in, I think C.4.14 … We were great friends. If you know him give it to him from C.3.3.'

In March 1898 Oscar sent a long letter to the *Daily Chronicle* attacking the treatment of prisoners. 'The present prison system seems almost to have as its aim the wrecking and the destruction of the mental faculties,' he wrote. 'The production of insanity, if not its intention, is certainly its result.' Wilde's letter suggested a number of reforms to improve the diet, hygiene and sleeping conditions of prisoners, and criticized the role of prison staff ('the most difficult task is to humanize the governors of prisons, to civilize the warders and to Christianize the chaplains'). The letter was published on the day that the House of Commons began debating the Prison Act, which introduced many of the reforms it suggested. Oscar's comments may have played a small part in helping to secure its safe passage through Parliament.

Oscar Wilde regained his freedom on the morning of 19 May 1898, having served his two-year sentence in full. On 18 May he left Reading for Pentonville prison, where he was to be issued his release papers on the following morning. Before Oscar departed Governor Nelson gave him a bulky package containing the manuscript of 'De Profundis'. Oscar would not re-read it, but instead gave the unopened letter to Robbie Ross when he met him again. Oscar was wearing his ordinary clothes to spare him the embarrassment he had experienced during his transfer from Wandsworth in 1895, and the journey went quietly. At 6.15a.m. on the next morning he walked out of the gates of Pentonville, where Stewart Headlam and More Adey were waiting with a cab. They took him to Headlam's house, where a number of his closest friends called to greet him over the next few hours. Wilde had aged noticeably and was much thinner as a result of his prison experiences. Yet one small incident on the previous day suggested his ebullient spirit was not fully extinguished. At Twyford Station, whilst he waited with his warders for the London train, Oscar suddenly opened wide his

163

arms towards some flowering shrubbery, and then cried out: 'Oh Beautiful World! Oh Beautiful World!' His guards were shocked and warned him: 'Now Mr Wilde, you mustn't give yourself away like that. You're the only man in England who would talk like that in a railway station.'

CHAPTER XI

*T*HE FINAL YEARS

There was no place in England for Oscar now, and on the afternoon of his release he took the ferry to Dieppe in France. He found Robbie Ross and Reggie Turner waiting on the pier. They had raised £800 for him from his friends and sympathizers, which would remove his immediate financial worries. Oscar booked into a hotel in the town under a pseudonym, and settled down to adjust to his exile. Within a few days he received a placatory letter from Douglas, which stated that the young man's feelings towards him had not changed and asked for a meeting. Oscar's profound distaste for Bosie had softened after writing 'De Profundis', but he had not abandoned his hopes of reconciling himself with Constance. His immediate desire, however, was to exorcize his prison experiences with a long poem he had in mind. Oscar settled down to write 'The Ballad of Reading Gaol', a work that he intended to be both a critique of England's penal system and a testimony to his own suffering over the previous three years.

Most of the 'Ballad' was written between 7 July and 20 July 1897, although Oscar revised it and added some extra stanzas later in the year. The verse pattern and much of the poem's imagery were closely modelled on Coleridge's 'Rime of the Ancient Mariner'. Oscar took as his theme a harrowing event that had taken place whilst he was in Reading Gaol, namely the hanging of Trooper Charles Thomas Wooldridge on 7 July 1896. The soldier's crime was the murder of his wife in a fit of jealous rage, as Oscar pointed out in its first stanza.

> 'He did not wear his scarlet coat
> For blood and wine are red
> And blood and wine were on his hands
> When they found him with the dead,
> The poor dead woman whom he loved
> And murdered in her bed.'

In fact Wooldridge did not kill his separated wife in bed, but cut her throat in a street in Windsor after pursuing her from the cottage where she was hiding from him. Nor, for that matter, did he own a scarlet coat, since his unit, the Royal Horse Guards, wore blue. But such minor details were irrelevant to the 'Ballad'. Its best parts are those dealing with Wooldridge's state of mind and the reactions of his fellow prisoners and the prison staff to the impending execution.

> 'The governor was strong upon
> The Regulation Act;
> The doctor said that death was but
> A scientific fact;
> And twice a day the chaplain called
> And left a little tract.'

But in writing about Woodridge's execution, Oscar was also drawing a parallel with his own situation.

166

> 'A prison wall was round us both
> Two outcast men we were
> The world has thrust us from its heart
> And God from out His care
> And the iron gin that waits for sin
> Had caught us in its snare.'

It is through this autobiographical quality, along with the compassionate portrayal of the murderer as society's scapegoat, that the 'Ballad' transcends its many faults. Half propaganda and half personal pleading, Wilde's last poem still has the power to move the reader with its sincerity and anguish of spirit. A somewhat disreputable publisher named Leonard Smithers ('the most learned pornographer in Europe') was persuaded to issue an edition of 'The Ballad of Reading Gaol' in February of the following year. He was the only person in England willing to print a book by the infamous Oscar Wilde. The 'Ballad' was published under the pseudonym C.3.3 but the true identity of its author was an open secret. The book, his last published work, was a runaway success and sold 4,000 copies within a year. A small de luxe edition of ninety-nine copies, with the author's real name on the title page, was also printed. Oscar sent many of these to the friends and fellow writers who had not turned on him during his trial and imprisonment.

There was one repeated stanza in the ballad that drew a parallel between Wooldridge's crime and the betrayal that had caused his own disgrace.

> 'Yet each man kills the thing he loves,
> By each let this be heard,

> Some do it with a bitter look,
> Some with a flattering word,
> The coward does it with a kiss,
> The brave man with a sword!'

Oscar, despite all that had happened between them, was still drawn to Bosie, especially since there was no sign of Constance taking him back. Within weeks of his release the two men were again exchanging affectionate letters. Oscar was annoyed that Douglas had given interviews about him in France, but was prepared to forgive the indiscretion. The lovers planned that Douglas would come secretly to Dieppe, where Oscar was living under the name of Sebastian Melmoth, but had to abandon the idea when word slipped out to Constance. Instead, in the last week of August 1897, Oscar went to Rouen and spent the night there with Bosie. Afterwards he sent him a long telegram: '... Everyone is furious with me for going back to you, but they don't understand us. I feel that it is only with you that I can do anything at all. Do remake my ruined life for me, and then our friendship and love will have a different meaning to the world.'

Six weeks later they met again in Aix-le-Bains and travelled onwards to Naples. Oscar and Bosie were planning to spend the winter together, but the reunion was a failure from beginning to end. It was madness on both men's parts to think their bond could have survived the events of the previous three years. Bosie had received a copy of Oscar's long letter to him from Robbie Ross, but having been warned of its painful contents burnt the manuscript without reading it. He would accept no responsibility for the harm he had caused by his selfishness, whilst Oscar was still haunted by the traumas of his fall and imprisonment. Fate eventually intervened to separate the unhappy couple. Constance Wilde and Lady Queensberry were both eager to bring a permanent end to the liaison, even if for different reasons. To achieve this aim they decided to exert financial pressure on the lovers. Constance, furious that her husband had broken his word by returning to Douglas, cut off his allowance of £150 a year. At the same time Lady Queensberry threatened to do the same thing to Bosie, who had very little income of his own. In addition she offered to pay the pair's debts in Naples, and to give Oscar £200 if he severed all connections with her son.

In early December 1897 Douglas removed himself from Naples, leaving Oscar behind; the parting took place in an atmosphere of financial wrangling and mutual distrust. The re-kindled alliance had not even survived until Christmas. 'Bosie for four months, by endless letters, offered me a home.' Oscar wrote. 'He offered me love, affection and care, and promised that I should never want for anything. But when we met on our way to Naples I found that he had no money, no plans, and had forgotten all his promises. When my allowance ceased he left.' He would retain an uneasy friendship with Douglas until his death, but their romantic attachment was over for good.

With Bosie permanently off the scene, Wilde tried to re-build his bridges with Constance, who was now living in Genoa. But it was too late. He had ceased to be his wife's chief concern, for the chronic back injury from which she suffered was causing unendurable pain. In the spring of 1898 Constance entered hospital to have it operated on. The surgeons could not help her, and she died on 7 April, at the age of forty. In her will Constance generously provided for her husband's annual allowance of £150 a year to continue, but she forbade him ever to see his sons again. Oscar's feelings at the death of his wife were ambivalent. He was still a practising homosexual, and with Bosie had eagerly pursued youths in Naples, yet Constance represented a safe haven in a world that had no place for him. 'My way to hope and a new life ends in her grave,' he told Frank Harris. In the following year Oscar stopped off in Genoa to visit the burial place of the woman who had paid such a high price for her loyalty to him. 'I went to Genoa to see Constance's grave,' he wrote to Robert Ross.

'It is very pretty – a marble cross with dark ivy leaves inlaid in a good pattern ... It was very tragic seeing her name carved on a tomb – her surname, my name not mentioned of course – just "Constance Mary, daughter of Horace Lloyd Q.C." and a verse from Revelations. I brought some flowers. I was deeply affected – with a sense also of the uselessness of all regrets. Nothing could have been otherwise and life is a very terrible thing.'

In 1898 Oscar left Italy and moved back Paris, where he would spend most of the short spell of life left to him. There was little left now of the brilliant peacock who once moved so gloriously through London high society, save only the occasional flash of wit. Wilde had grown fat and seedy, and the immaculate aesthete of earlier years had become a tubby giant in dishevelled clothes who smelt of the absinthe he consumed at all hours of the day. Following 'The Ballad of Reading Gaol' his literary output dried up, and the only work he undertook was correcting the proofs of the texts of 'An Ideal Husband' and 'The Importance of Being Earnest', which Leonard Smithers published in 1899. 'The intense energy of creation has been kicked out of me,' he said, and 'I can write, but I have lost the joy of writing.' Oscar was not above accepting advances for projected works, but he knew they would never see the light of day. His friends tried to help, and at the end of 1898 Frank Harris brought him to the Riviera for three months. He hoped a change of air might encourage Oscar to write again, but it was a waste of energy. The talent that had produced a string of stories, essays, poems and plays in the decade before 1895 was dormant, and could not be awakened. Wilde drank absinthe and pursued the young fishermen in the small coastal villages around Cannes, but he wrote nothing more than a few of his eloquent letters. 'I told you I was going to write something,' he told Laurence Housman, the author of children's fairy tales, '... but in my heart – that chamber of leaden echoes – I know that I never shall.'

Money remained one of Oscar's main preoccupations. The allowance from Constance's estate should have kept him in modest circumstances, but he was extravagant. He shamelessly cadged and borrowed wherever he could, living on credit in hotels until they lost patience with him, and then moving on again. Oscar hoped he might once again make substantial sums from his writings, but it was a pipe dream. 'Still I keep on building castles of fairy gold in the air; we Celts always do,' he wrote to Ernest Dowson. In Paris and on the Riviera he was often seen by his former London acquaintances. As often as not they snubbed him. Even George Alexander, whose St James's theatre had been made with

'Lady Windermere's Fan', turned away when they met by chance in Cannes. Later he made amends by returning the copyright of the two Wilde plays he owned to their author without any charge. André Gide met Oscar by accident in a boulevard café in Paris. 'I am so alone these days,' he told the French novelist. They had a long conversation, but Gide only saw him once again. Another friend of many years standing, the English opera singer Dame Nellie Melba, was shocked when Oscar staggered up one day on the street, identified himself, and then asked for some money.

In February 1899 Wilde accepted an invitation from Harold Mellor, an Englishman he had met on the Riviera, to stay at his villa on Lake Geneva in Switzerland. He disliked Mellor ('he is unsocial, taciturn, wretched company') and hated Switzerland: 'Swiss people are carved out of wood with a rough knife, most of them; the others are carved out of turnip,' he wrote to Ross. The penniless author was stranded with his mean host for over a month before he was able to raise some money and escape to Italy. During his Swiss interlude Oscar received news of the death of Willie Wilde – 'my poor dear brother who could compromise a steam engine'. He could not find it in his heart to mourn for the coarse Willie, who had treated him with such unkindness in the weeks leading up to the trial, although he felt sorry for his widow, Lily. Oscar was back in Paris by the summer of 1899, where he proceeded to run up huge debts that he could not afford to pay. By August he was on the verge of being thrown out on the street by the manager of the Marsollier hotel. He was rescued from this ignominy by Jean Dupoirier, the owner of the nearby Hotel d'Alsace, who cleared his bill and offered him a room on credit in his establishment. Wilde, saved from destitution, moved into his benefactor's hotel, where he was to stay until his death.

On 31 January 1900, the Marquess of Queensberry died at the age of fifty-six, bequeathing a substantial fortune to his surviving sons. Lord Alfred went to Paris to celebrate the demise of his unlamented father, and treated his old lover to dinner. During the evening Oscar asked his now wealthy friend for financial help. Bosie responded by calling him an 'old whore', and announced 'I can't afford to spend anything except upon myself.' His ingratitude was all the more offensive considering the vast sums of Oscar's money consumed by him during their years together. The older man felt humiliated and profoundly offended at Bosie's mean-spirited attitude, but there was nothing he could do about it. Perhaps by now Oscar was used to rejection over money, since his constant scrabbling for loans and advances had already led to arguments with his publisher Leonard Smithers and many of his oldest friends.

In April 1900 Wilde enjoyed one last trip to Italy, when he accompanied the despised Harold Mellor to Palermo in Sicily. On his way home he visited Rome, where he encountered his old flame John Gray by accident on the street. Gray was now studying to be a priest and would not acknowledge his presence. On Holy Thursday a stranger walked up and presented Oscar with a ticket to an audience in the Vatican. He attended the ceremony, and was blessed by Pope Leo XIII. Mellor's departure for Switzerland allowed Wilde to spend a few days in the company of Omerto, a young 'guide' whose name Robbie Ross had passed on to him. Wilde had taken up photography, and observed in his letters to Ross that '… in my moments of depression (alas!! Not rare) I think

173

that I was intended to be a photographer', and 'Cows are very fond of being photographed, and unlike architecture don't move'. After leaving the pleasures of Rome behind he visited Constance's grave in Genoa, and then stayed for ten days with Mellor on Lake Geneva before returning to the Hotel d'Alsace.

As the summer of 1900 progressed into autumn, Oscar's health began to decline rapidly. Wandsworth and Reading Gaol had permanently impaired him physically, whilst the long years of heavy drinking, chain smoking and rich food were now taking a heavy toll on his vitality. Wilde was covered in a blotchy red rash that he attributed to 'mussel poisoning', although its real cause was most likely neuralgia or the long-term effects of syphilis. By September he was weakening badly and took to his bed, just like his father Sir William in his last months. Oscar's recurring ear infection, the legacy of his fall in the prison chapel, was causing him great pain. Dr Tucker, the medical practitioner recommended by the British Embassy, initiated a series of uncomfortable daily treatments to drain the poison from the ear. He recommended an operation, which was carried out on 10 October, but it was not successful. Oscar telegraphed Robbie Ross: 'Terribly weak, please come.' When his brother's widow Lily came to visit the patient with her new husband, he told her: 'I am dying beyond my means. I will not outlive the century ... I cannot even afford to die.' Ross arrived in Paris on 16 October and found Oscar weak but in good spirits. He joked about their shared, sinful past: 'Ah Robbie, when we are dead and buried in our porphyry tombs, and the trumpet of the Last Judgement is sounded, I shall turn to you and whisper "Let us pretend we do not hear it". '

The attention he received from the friends who visited him rallied the lonely exile a little. Towards the end of October he felt well enough to go out with Ross and some others to have a glass of absinthe at a local tavern. 'My wallpaper and I are fighting to the death,' he told one of the company. 'One of us has to go.' But the improvement in his health was brief. A few days later he came down with a cold, and complained of an unbearable pain in his head. He was diagnosed as suffering from meningitis, the lingering result, Ross believed, of his bout of syphilis at Oxford. The sick man was clearly sinking to his death. In his moments of lucidity Oscar asked Ross (who with Reginald Turner was almost constantly at his bedside) to settle his debts and to do his best to have 'De Profundis' published. He talked about his children, and when Turner tried to nurse him complained that he should be a doctor, 'as you always want people to do what they don't want to'.

Oscar, even on his sickbed, was pursuing another dispute over money, this time with Frank Harris. Realizing that the Irishman would never write again, Harris had offered to work up a play based on one of Wilde's old plots. Oscar agreed to share the royalties, and the completed play was staged in 1900 as 'Mr and Mrs Daventry'. Harris was supposed to pay an advance of £150 to his co-author, but he found that Oscar had secretly sold a share in the project to several other people. After they were paid off only a fraction of the promised advance remained. Wilde, desperately needing money for his operation, sent a number of letters demanding the full sum, even though his own behaviour was responsible for the situation. On 20 November 1900 he composed a long diatribe to Harris, unfairly blaming his

175

sickness on the 'mental anxiety' of not receiving the advance. It was the last letter Oscar ever wrote. Within the week he fell into a semi-conscious state, from which it was obvious he would not recover. Barely a month after his forty-sixth birthday, Oscar Wilde lay dying.

Ross had gone to the south of France with his mother, but he returned on the morning of 29 November, after Reggie Turner sent him an urgent telegram. He decided he should find a Catholic priest and have the writer received into the Catholic faith before it was too late. Ross ran to the nearby Passionist Monastery to look for one who could speak English, and returned to the Hotel d'Alsace with a Father Cuthbert Dunne. Since he had been a child, Oscar had been attracted to Catholicism. Now, expiring in the dingy bedroom of a cheap French hotel, he lifted his hand to ask for the Last Rites. Father Dunne baptized, anointed and absolved him. Oscar drifted back into unconsciousness, with Ross and Turner waiting beside the bed for the end. He lingered on till a few minutes before two o'clock on the afternoon of the following day, 30 November, when at last he died. M. Dupoirier, the hotel manager who had treated him so generously over the previous twelve months, dressed the corpse in a clean white shirt. Father Dunne wrapped a rosary around his hands and placed palm branches on his chest. A little later Maurice Gilbert, a young French soldier befriended by Oscar, arrived with a camera. At Ross's request he photographed the writer on his deathbed.

Oscar's friends could only afford a cheap 'sixth-class' funeral, with an old hearse and four ramshackle carriages. Douglas, freshly arrived from London, was amongst the fourteen mourners who attended the requiem Mass at the church of St Germain-des-Prés. Afterwards the funeral procession drove to the unfashionable cemetery at Bagneux, on the outskirts of Paris. Ireland's greatest writer of the nineteenth century was laid in the ground with little more fuss than the executed murderer whose burial he described so eloquently in 'The Ballad of Reading Gaol'. Only one minor incident enlivened the grim occasion. As the coffin was lowered, there was a scramble to get to the front of the small crowd of mourners, and Lord Alfred was nearly pushed into the open grave. Oscar Wilde – genius, author, wit and martyr – would have appreciated the irony.

ℐFTERWORD

News of Oscar's death reached England within hours, and on 1 December 1900 his obituary appeared in the London *Times*. 'The verdict that a jury passed upon his conduct at the Old Bailey in May 1895, destroyed for ever his reputation, and condemned him to ignoble obscurity for the remainder of his days ... Death has soon ended what must have been a life of wretchedness and unavailing regret.' For many years this would be the majority view on his life, yet Wilde was too important a figure in the cultural history of his era to be forgotten or ignored. In the years immediately after Oscar's death, Robbie Ross took on the unenviable role of his champion and literary executor. The first task he undertook was to clear the dead man's debts so his estate could be released from receivership. By 1906 Ross had achieved this aim, and was able to retrieve Wilde's copyrights for his children Cyril and Vivian, who had now taken the name of Holland.

In 1905 Ross published the short version of 'De Profundis', which omitted all references to Douglas. Despite the removal of this material, the edited text hinted that the relationship had been intimate and deeply harmful to Oscar's interests. Lord Alfred had renounced his homosexuality soon after Wilde's death; he married in 1902 and converted to Catholicism in 1911. Now he was adamant that there had never been an intimate attachment between himself and Oscar, and threatened legal action every time the issue was raised in articles and books. In 1912, following the publication of a biography by Arthur Ransome, Douglas took out a libel case, and the whole of the contentious letter was read out in court as evidence. Bosie heard Oscar's devastating criticisms of his actions, character and literary talents for the first time; he was not able to bear them and stormed out of the courtroom. He retaliated for his humiliation by persecuting Ross in a fashion reminiscent of his father's hounding of Wilde. His victim was eventually driven to sue him for libel, but the court case caused more harm to his own reputation than the defendant's. Ross escaped prosecution afterwards, but the anxiety caused by the public attacks of Douglas contributed to his comparatively early death in 1918.

Douglas never really escaped from the shadow of his relationship with Oscar, which pursued him throughout his life. In his later years he became a mirror image of his father, and was involved in a series of sordid personal mishaps and public controversies. Bosie's marriage ended in a messy and unpleasant divorce, and in 1923 he spent six months in prison for criminally libelling Winston Churchill. Whilst serving his sentence he composed a sonnet sequence, 'In Excelsis', his answer to Oscar's 'De Profundis'; like his other poetry it is virtually forgotten today. In his later years Douglas became as homophobic as his father, and dedicated himself 'to exposing and smashing Wilde's cult and the Wilde myth'. In his earlier accounts of the affair (published in *Oscar Wilde and Myself* and his *Autobiography*), Bosie portrayed Wilde as an evil moral influence, and lied about his own earlier homosexuality. In 1940, however, he wrote a more generous account of his former friend in *Oscar Wilde: A Summing Up*.

When Lord Alfred died in 1945, his *Times* obituary described him as 'a poet of distinction', but posterity remembers him solely for his intimacy with Oscar Wilde.

It was never Ross's intention to leave Oscar's body in the cemetery of Bagneux. In 1909 the writer's remains were exhumed, and re-interred at the more august Père-Lachaise cemetery in Paris. Ross, with money donated by Lady Carew, purchased a magnificent Jacob Epstein sculpture of a winged angel for the tomb. On the monument, beneath Oscar's name, four lines from 'The Ballad of Reading Gaol' were inscribed.

> 'And Alien tears will fill for him
> Pity's long broken urn,
> For his mourners will be outcast men
> And outcasts always mourn.'

In death, as in life, Ross wished his star to be tied to that of his mentor, friend and occasional lover. In 1950 his request to be buried with Wilde was finally honoured, and his ashes were re-interred in the tomb at Père-Lachaise. Thirteen years later, in 1963, the words 'Wife of Oscar Wilde' were added to Constance's headstone in Genoa. Oscar's two children were to have very different fates. Cyril, his beloved elder son, volunteered to fight in the First World War, and died in action in 1915. Vivian, on the other hand, followed his father's trade and became a respected writer under the name of Vivian Holland.

The revival of Oscar Wilde's reputation, both literary and personal, was a gradual process. The writer, as opposed to the man, was soon brought out of the shadows.

His plays and other works, with the single exception of the withheld sections of 'De Profundis', were soon made available to the public again. But Oscar's personal reputation was not fully restored until attitudes towards homosexuality relaxed in Britain, around 1960. Many biographies and memoirs of Wilde were published in the decades after his death – from Robert Sherard's 1906 'Life', to Frank Harris's racy *His Life and Confessions* in 1916, and Hesketh Pearson's classic account in 1946. Yet a whiff of sulphur was still attached to Oscar's name in England, if not in other countries. In France, where it was generally felt that only a nation of homosexuals could be as homophobic as the English, the sexual peccadilloes of a famous writer were not considered very important. The Irish, who rather like their literary heroes to have a disreputable side, felt much the same way.

A turning point in the public rehabilitation of Oscar in England came in 1960, when two films based on H. Montgomery Hyde's 1954 account of *The Trials of Oscar Wilde* were released within days of each other. Their respective leading men, Robert Morley and Peter Finch, portrayed Oscar sympathetically, as the victim of a prejudiced law; both films laid the blame for his imprisonment on Queensberry and Bosie. In that same year the great actor Micheál Mac Liammoir first appeared in his one-man show, 'The Importance of Being Oscar', which brought the wit and charming conversation of his fellow Irishman to audiences throughout the world; Mac Liammoir performed his stage show on 1,384 occasions before his retirement in 1975. The *Letters of Oscar Wilde*, published in 1962, formed another milestone. They presented the most inti-

181

mate picture of Oscar that had yet been published, and offered a deeper insight into the see-saw love affair with Bosie that led to his downfall. Today Wilde stands higher in the pantheon of British and Irish writers than at any time since his death, and he is acknowledged as one of the most brilliant and paradoxical intellects of the nineteenth century.

CHRONOLOGY

1854 Oscar Fingal O'Flahertie Wills Wilde born on October 16 at 21 Westland Row, Dublin – the son of William Wilde and Jane Francesca Wilde (nee Elgee), the poet 'Speranza'.

1864 Oscar and his elder brother Willie attend Portora School, County Down. His parents are sued in the Mary Travers libel case.

1867 Death of Isola Wilde, Oscar's nine-year-old sister.

1869 Oscar wins the Carpenter Prize for Greek scripture.

1870 Enters Trinity College, Dublin. His tutor is the eminent scholar J. P. Mahaffy.

1874 Wins the Berkeley Gold Medal for Greek. Is awarded a scholarship to Magdalen College, Oxford.

1875 Publishes his first poem, in Dublin.

1876 Death of Sir William Wilde. Oscar falls in love with Florence Balcombe.

1877 Visits Italy and Greece with Mahaffy. Audience with Pope Pius XI in Rome.

1878 Wins Newdigate Prize for poem 'Ravenna'. Completes double First degree at Oxford.

1879 Moves to London, where he shares a house with Frank Miles.

1881 'Poems' published.

1882 Spends most of the year on lecture tour of United States and Canada.

1883 Forms friendship with Robert Sherard in Paris. Returns to New York for premiere of the play 'Vera'.

1884 Marries Constance Lloyd. The couple honeymoon in Paris, where Oscar reads Huysman's *A Rebours*. Wilde buys and furnishes a house in Tite Street, Chelsea.

1885 First son, Cyril Wilde, born.

1886 Second son, Vivian Wilde, born. Oscar meets Robert (Robbie) Ross and forms his first known homosexual relationship.

1887 Appointed editor of *Woman's World*.

1888 Publishes *The Happy Prince and Other Stories*.

1889 Publishes 'Pen Pencil and Poison', 'The Decay of Lying', and 'The Portrait of Mr W. H.'

1890 *The Picture of Dorian Gray* published in *Lippincott's Monthly Magazine*.

1891 Visits Paris, where he meets Mallarm and André Gide. Publishes 'Critic As Artist', *The Picture of Dorian Gray* (as book), 'The Soul of Man Under Socialism', *Lord Arthur Savile's Crime and Other Stories* and *The House of Pomegranates*. 'The Duchess of Padua' is staged in New York as 'Guido Ferranti'. Introduced to Lord Alfred Douglas by Lionel Johnson.

1892 'Lady Windermere's Fan' is staged at the St James's Theatre. 'Salome' banned by Lord Chamberlain's office. Wilde begins his affair with Lord Alfred Douglas.

1893 'A Woman of No Importance' is staged at the Haymarket Theatre, London. 'Salome' (French language edition) published in Paris and London. Douglas goes to Egypt after he quarrels with Oscar.

1894 Douglas returns and is reconciled with Wilde in Paris. His father, the Marquess of Queensberry, confronts Wilde in his Tite Street house. Wilde plans to break with Douglas after they quarrel in Brighton, but is deterred by the suicide of Lord Drumlanrig. The English translation of 'Salome' (with illustrations by Aubrey Beardsley) is published. The poem 'The Sphinx' is published.

1895 'An Ideal Husband' and 'The Importance of Being Earnest' are staged (January and February). Queensberry leaves a card for 'Oscar Wilde posing as a Sodomite' at the Albermarle Club (18 February). Wilde takes a libel case, and is exposed as a homosexual under cross-examination by Edward Carson. He is arrested afterwards (3–5 April). Auction of Wilde's possessions at Tite Street (24 April). First trial on indecency charges ends with jury failing to agree a verdict (26 April–1 May). At second trial is convicted with Alfred Taylor and sentenced to two years' hard labour (22 May–25 May). Begins sentence in Pentonville Prison. Declared bankrupt. Moved to Wandsworth Prison; injures his ear in a fall and is confined to the infirmary for two months. Transferred to Reading Gaol (November).

1896 Death of Lady Wilde in London (February). Execution of Charles Thomas Wooldridge (inspiration for 'Ballad of Reading Gaol'). 'Salome' produced in Paris.

1897 Writes the letter to Douglas usually known as 'De Profundis' (January–March). Released from prison

(May). Leaves England for France, where he stays in Dieppe under the pseudonym Sebastian Melmoth. Meets Douglas and goes with him to Naples, but the reunion fails.

1898 'Ballad of Reading Gaol' published under pseudonym C.3.3. Constance Wilde dies in Genoa (April). Oscar travels to the French Riviera with Frank Harris.

1899 'The Importance of Being Earnest' and 'An Ideal Husband' published by Leonard Smithers. Oscar stays in Switzerland with Harold Mellor. Death of Willie Wilde in London. Oscar visits the grave of Constance Wilde. He moves into the Hotel d'Alsace, Paris.

1900 The Marquess of Queensberry dies. Wilde visits Sicily and Rome, where he is blessed by Pope Leo XIII. Operation on infected ear in Paris (10 October). Takes to his bed, and is nursed by Robbie Ross and Reggie Turner. Develops meningitis, probably the long-term result of syphilis (November). Received into the Catholic faith by Father Cuthbert Dunne (29 November). Dies just before two o'clock on the afternoon of 30 November in the Hotel d'Alsace, Paris, aged forty-six. Wilde is buried in the Cemetery of Bagneux (3 December). Mourners include Douglas, Ross and Turner.

1905 Part of Wilde's prison letter published as 'De

Profundis'. Strauss's opera 'Salome', using Wilde's text as libretto, is staged in Berlin.

1906 Ross discharges Wilde's bankruptcy. Robert Sherard publishes first biography of Oscar Wilde.

1909 Wilde's remains are moved to Père-Lachaise cemetery and buried under a monument by the sculptor Jacob Epstein.

1915 Cyril Holland, Wilde's eldest son, killed in the First World War.

1918 Death of Robert Ross, Wilde's friend and literary executor.

1931 'Salome' receives its first public performance in England, at the Lyceum Theatre, London.

1945 Death of Lord Alfred Douglas.

1950 Ross's ashes placed in Wilde's tomb.

1962 *The Letters of Oscar Wilde* published, including the full text of 'De Profundis'.

2000 Centenary of the death of Oscar Wilde.